T0193337

Denise Devlin

The Untold Story

Peter and Jesus – The Gap Years

BALBOA.
PRESS

A DIVISION OF HAY HOUSE

Balboa Press books may be ordered through booksellers or by contacting:

Balboa Press
A Division of Hay House
1663 Liberty Drive
Bloomington, IN 47403
www.balboapress.com
1 (877) 407-4847

Because of the dynamic nature of the Internet, any web addresses or links contained in this book may have changed since publication and may no longer be valid. The views expressed in this work are solely those of the author and do not necessarily reflect the views of the publisher, and the publisher hereby disclaims any responsibility for them.

The author of this book does not dispense medical advice or prescribe the use of any technique as a form of treatment for physical, emotional, or medical problems without the advice of a physician, either directly or indirectly. The intent of the author is only to offer information of a general nature to help you in your quest for emotional and spiritual well-being. In the event you use any of the information in this book for yourself, which is your constitutional right, the author and the publisher assume no responsibility for your actions.

Any people depicted in stock imagery provided by Getty Images are models, and such images are being used for illustrative purposes only. Certain stock imagery © Getty Images.

Print information available on the last page.

ISBN: 978-1-9822-0101-2 (sc)
ISBN: 978-1-9822-0102-9 (hc)
ISBN: 978-1-9822-0124-1 (e)

Library of Congress Control Number: 2018903683

Balboa Press rev. date: 05/03/2018

Contents

St Peter and Jesus' dialogue:
And messages of Peter's friendship with Jesus.
How they met and spent the years before the
ministry of spreading the Word of God.

Here are the truths of a time that
have never before been told.
They are enlightening, inspiring and full of love,
With St Peter as witness, he tells of how it really was,
How Jesus and God come from only
a place of unconditional love.

Acknowledgements

I would like to thank the many soulful people who supported me during the scribing and along the path to publishing this book.

My friend Mary Howick, you were there for the first arm movement and never doubted my calling. The significance of the date the 18th November, began on that February day 2017. Thank you.

Sinead Lynch for your continual love, support and intuitive guidance, especially when I'd get *'into my head.'* Much gratitude for the beautiful pen that you gifted me for scribing and we just love how the ink ran out during the last sentence. As we always say *"You couldn't make it up."*

To my school pal Noelle Donnell for the coffee meet ups, support and first proof read.

Ciaran Corr for second and subsequent proof reads, plus editorial content and review, and doing all your magic so quickly to get it to Balboa Press. You were the manifestation of my thoughts for an editor, this wouldn't have happened without you, much gratitude indeed.

To Kathy Weiss, meeting you in Denver September 2017 was the reason I was there, not for Positive Parties 'Training with A Difference' as I had originally thought! Thank you for channelling the title.

Aideen McGinley for your wisdom, friendship, guidance, encouragement, for trusting my synchronicities and connecting me with Marsha at Balboa Press.

To my childhood best friend Kerry-Anne O'Donnell for all your love, support and taking my photograph for this book.

To Brian and Mary Mooney for the loan of Foxlodge's beautiful garden for the photo shoot. And to their daughter, my wise, witty, wonderful school friend and soul sister Fiona Mooney, who left this earth on the 20th May 2016. I truly miss your physical presence Fi, yet I always feel your beautiful spirit guiding me along my journey. Keep sending me those signs Fi, I am comforted and inspired by every one.

To all the friends I trusted to tell about this channelling. Many of you believed me and didn't think I was going mad! Others did think I had *'lost the plot'* yet you loved and supported me anyway. I did originally list you all to thank you personally but in fear of leaving anyone out I am just going to say a great big thank you, you know who you are and I appreciate your friendship, love and support always.

The McGrane family - my parents, brothers, sisters-in-law and nieces and all the Devlin family - my mother-in-law, brothers and sisters-in-law and their families for their love and support. In this family unit, some of you *'get'* channelling and others don't, but you have all been supporting me regardless, for that I am very thankful.

Last, but not least, my own rock - my husband Neil - who believes, loves and supports me throughout my journey. I am so blessed to have you as my soul mate and I love you always. You are a loving spiritual man. Little did we know when you handed me 'Conversations With God' on our first date, and it took me seven years to actually be in place to read it, that I too would be channel 17 years later.

And our gorgeous girls, Emer and Orla who, in relation to this channelling, looked after me in public places and would always hold my arm down when it would shake uncontrollably in front of others. Thank you, my three darlings, for believing in me, you saw this gift as normal and never for a moment questioned this channelling role.

And, lastly to St Peter, so much gratitude for this wonderful gift. It was truly an honour to scribe for you.

Introduction

I am Peter - Simon Peter - as Jesus called me. I am telling my story as it has never been told before. This is the truth; the whole truth which has been hidden from the people. But now is a time of Higher Consciousness and the world is ready and not only wants to, but needs to know.

I have chosen to come through an ordinary woman, not an ordained priest or Holy Person but someone who has lived, sinned and fallen on and off her path. The churches will not be too pleased to hear this. Men of the cloth will cry out "why not me?" and I reply, "because God's word is for everybody, not just the holy ones, seen to be in the church and taking an active role." Many people all over the planet are now choosing to live in Higher Consciousness without attending any formal religious institutions. There is much freedom gained from self-discovery of God and coming to love and accepting your true being because you have had the trial and tribulations which bring you to discovering the deepness that lies within you, which is actually Source/Spirit/God.

My role in this story is to tell you Jesus/Yeshua spoke of love and how his teachings, although scribed well, have become indoctrinated by the churches with many man-made rules and regulations.

Only now are people waking up to this. Even this Pope St Francis, who is Christ-like and has many qualities of St Francis of Assisi, is making changes and causing ripples in the Roman Catholic Church.

By coming through an ordinary woman, mother, wife, to scribe this book, this breaks down barriers to the normal channelling that the churches, especially the Catholic Church, are used to.

I will use simple language and keep my story clear and to the point. This will be for all, all ages, all religions. ALL. Even those who may not believe may come to know that this is true. I am true to my word.

I am Peter, Simon Peter of Galilee, I was a fisherman and an apostle of Jesus Christ.

Friendship

I first met Jesus when I was a boy. I didn't know who he was but he stood out like a lone star in the sky. He was bright, serene, calm and peaceful, like no other child I had ever met. He was with his mother at the time. She called on him and he looked at her with such love. I always remember that. They were in the market buying fruit and fish. I was with my father and had just come off the boat with our catch. I was a few years older, so I thought I was wiser in my years. I showed off by swaying when I walked as if to say *'look at me out fishing like a man and you are just a boy.'* We were both 13 and 16 at the time. My voice was like a man's, his still had to break. I remember hearing that when he spoke to his mother. He spoke with such gentleness too.

They both wanted to buy some of our fish - herring, they wanted - but we had none, only sole. I remember he smiled at me while my father and Mary spoke. Little did I know how I would be affected by him and come to love him and his mother Mary in years to come.

We did not speak but his presence made an impact on me. It was when I met him years later and he called on me to join him, he said he knew that day in May that I would become his rock.

Denise Devlin

I was to become Jesus' rock in the most peculiar of ways about ten years later at a family birthday. Cousins of ours on both sides were related and we were invited. At that stage I was married to Sarah, we had a son and a child on the way. Jesus was with his mother Mary again, at that stage he was about 23. Again, his stature was striking, he smiled at everyone when they came in, I knew him immediately, I remembered his energy. The boy was now a man and his presence was felt by everyone. No one seemed to know how or why they were drawn to him, they just were. His eyes met your gaze when you looked at him and he only seemed to have eyes for you. He was truly present with everyone he spoke to, listening to their every word and tuning into their feelings. It was empathy in excellence and I had never witnessed this ever before.

It was at this family occasion we first spoke. I was introduced to Jesus by an uncle who said, "you two men could go into selling your wares together, good furniture and fresh fish are hard to come by, it would be a match made in heaven," and he laughed. Jesus then held out his two hands towards me, beckoned me to take his and he looked at me with his twinkling eyes and said, "what do you think Simon or may I call you Peter?" "But I am called Simon," I answered.

"You may be," he replied, smiling, "but to me you look like a Peter." If anyone else had dared to change my name I would have been angry and challenged them but with Jesus I knew it was meant to be. So, from then on, and I don't know how or why, but everyone referred to me as Simon Peter or simply just Peter.

The rest of the evening we talked and laughed as if we were long lost brothers. I could tell that the energy between us was special. We had a bond that no others had in the room, and it was like we just *'clicked,'* - a modern-day word, I know - but it is how I describe our bonding encounter.

We arranged to meet the next day, before the Sabbath. We met in Galilee and had food in a local tavern. Jesus told me many stories of his childhood, including his father Joseph and his mother Mary. He said he knew they had sacrificed a lot for him and he wanted to be able to look after his mother well. He felt that I could help do this, as he trusted me, even though we had just met. He said he remembered meeting me ten years before by the market and we hadn't spoke, as teenage boys are so emotionally shy at that age. He said he knew from that day that we would meet again and begin a journey together.

Now most men don't meet another man at a family gathering, become firm friends and agree the next day to look after one's mother. It was extremely strange but very normal at the same time. How could I say anything but yes? This man was magical and to be in his presence was truly magnificent. I knew that I was in the presence of the Son of God. At that moment I dropped to my knees in the tavern, took his two hands in mine and said: "Master, whatever you wish, I am here for you." Jesus replied, "get up Peter, sit with me like an equal. Yes, I am the Son of God and I know you realise this as you have been chosen to be an apostle - the leader of them all - but for now, we will eat and drink as brothers. I have some years yet before I start my ministry work for my Father in Heaven. Meanwhile, I want to be a carpenter, just as you are a fisherman. I wish us to be brothers and sell our wares together and support each other. I want to live like a man before my duties of truly teaching begins. Can we do this? Can we be brothers?"

I smiled, I broke bread, handed it to Jesus and said, "take this and eat with me brother, we will live like kings and then our mission will begin when you say so. Until then we will work, eat and play, and pray, for there will be wonderful opportunities for both of us.

So, we set up a business together. I would catch fish, Jesus would make furniture, do carvings and generally be very creative with wood. We linked the two trades by telling people about each other, a referral I suppose, but these days it would be called *'good networking.'*

We'd meet for breakfast twice a week, once at my home and then at his. This bi-weekly ritual became something to look forward to and cherish.

At my home, Sarah would cook for us and Jesus always helped clear the table and do the dishes. When he first did this I said, "sit down Jesus, that's women's work." He was quick to reply, "and why do you say that Simon Peter? Is your wife not equal to you? Why would you think it is not becoming of you or any man to help the women in the home?" I lowered my eyes in shame as he had not chastised me before. He continued "without women, my mother, your mother, we would not be here on this earth. Neither would your son nor your new child, who is in Sarah's womb, have a chance to come and experience this world. Therefore, we men must realise that fact and think more clearly before we speak of superiority, just because we are physically stronger. Women must be respected and treated equally for they are crucial to our very existence and have to be appreciated and honoured. Women can do everything men can do and more, they can bear children, which is a generous gift to the world. Women can and will be in all roles of life in society - politics, finance, farming, construction and within the church - including leadership roles. Why would they not be I ask you or anyone? So, Peter, I ask you again, do you think that clearing the table and doing the dishes is only women's work?"

I meekly looked at Jesus in the eyes and replied, "No."

Today I am also going to tell you how Jesus and I worked so well together. He had the wonderful gift of making people feel at ease with themselves. Some have the gift of making people feel at ease in their company, but this gift was unique in that people felt comfortable and safe in their own skins, so to speak. In his presence you felt safe, loved and lovable, that's why so many people flocked to him. Just to be in his company made them honour their Divine Light within, without them even realising why.

His gifts with people transcended into our business too. While folk felt the need for new furniture or wood carvings, once they were visiting him to make an order or collect an item, he would always mention me and how tasty my fresh fish were and how I had such a selection. I would be rushed off my feet once I brought my boat in with my catch. People would be waiting for me saying, "Jesus sent us, he says your fresh fish are delicious!"

One day he asked me if he could come fishing with me. "Of course," I said, "we'll take food and make a day of it. I'll put a notice by the dock to tell people I'll be in later than usual. Let's enjoy the day."

Jesus was like a little boy with a new toy that day. He was so delighted to be going out fishing with me. I had a new boat too, as my business was so good with all Jesus' referrals. I was able to replace my old boat with a new one. This was only my third time to use it. I was excited to be taking Jesus with me.

When we were out to sea about one hour, I cast the nets and Jesus helped me. He was so interested in how I set them up and cast them out. We also lifted some pots from the day before. It was a busy few hours before we sat and had lunch. Sarah had made us delicious bread with cheese and Jesus joked about how he hoped I'd helped and not just left it to *'the woman.'*

We talked about different things … our families, our hopes and dreams. It was that day that Jesus told me of his love for Mary Magdalene and how he hoped they would marry - she had been a childhood friend and sweetheart and she was very blessed with much Light. He said he knew his journey was not going to be an easy one and he was here on earth for a very specific purpose, but he knew her role would be huge in helping him reach his mission. He said he felt that people would not appreciate her role in his life and he knew he had to keep it low-key in order to keep her safe and protected. Again, he mentioned how women were equal to men, not inferior,

Denise Devlin

as many cultures portrayed. It may not be now but in years to come this would be realised by all. Some countries and cultures would embrace it, many others would not, but a time would come when the Divine Feminine would be vital to the earth and humanity.

Peter's Message
Cleansing of Male Egos and the Divine Feminine

When the rest of the world embraces the Divine Feminine, the world will be a very different place to be. For the sake of the future generations, this cleansing of male egos, power-hungry attitudes and competiveness has to happen now, especially in the churches and religious institutions that favour only men in the active roles. This has to stop. This is why people have veered away from churches in the past ten, twenty, thirty years. People who are becoming awakened and stepping into the Light can see the flaws of these religious institutions. There are, of course, many good men. However, how can the energy change when the Divine Feminine is not allowed to be part of the leadership, only allowed in the congregation? Yes, we see nuns in the Catholic Church but they are not permitted to say mass. Why ever not? If the Divine Feminine took an active role, you can guarantee a massive change in how people view the churches. Those who do have women in active services will vouch for this in their parishes, especially if the women are strong in their own feminine energy and not leaning over too much into their masculine aspect. This is what Jesus wanted for the world. 2,000 years later, he is still waiting.

2

Balance

Jesus and I continued our business partnership and friendship for many years before we actively went out on the ministry. Much of the teachings are recorded in the gospel yet those years before are rarely recorded, so here I tell some of the *'goings on'* between two friends and partners.

One day Jesus decided to ask Sarah to come to work with him in his workshop. He said he had seen a creative side to her in preparing food and arranging flowers so he knew that she would also be excellent at wood carvings as well. He felt she would have a flair for carpentry. All she had to do was learn the skills. Jesus told me that I had to stay home with our son Joshua and mind our new baby Maria, only bringing her over if she needed nursed. I smiled at his orders, knowing that although we were such close friends, the role of master and apostle would be arriving soon enough, so I might as well get used to his leadership requests.

Sarah was delighted to be asked to do something different with her creativity and it was just not the done thing for a woman to learn a trade. I left them to it and enjoyed the day spent with my two children. Joshua played and Maria slept most of the day as she was only a few months old. I had to bring her over a few times to Sarah to be nursed and I observed Jesus look at the sight of Sarah nursing Maria with such admiration and love. "Look Peter," he said, "how can it be that women can bear our children and keep them alive and grow with their own milk, yet men feel that they are better than them? It does not make any sense in my eyes, nor that of my Father. Why? Oh, why do such men not see the miracle created here and rejoice their beauty, bodies, characteristics and talents? I will show you today how your talented wife will create a wood-carving that would be proud to be built by a skilled carpenter.

I smiled, left them to it, and returned hours later when Maria needed nursed again. On my return Sarah was proudly holding a woodcarving of an owl. "Inner wisdom," she said, "that's what this owl stands for. I have always known I wanted to learn to work with wood. It's been there all along but I never knew I'd have the opportunity to try it. Peter, when I am carving, I feel the same happiness and joy I feel when I am nursing Maria. I know it's the same feelings when she suckles on me and her little hand is on my breast, and she looks at me with such love. It is the same feelings I felt today when Jesus showed me how to use the tools to carve the wood."

I looked into Sarah's eye and I noticed they were gleaming and twinkling, the same way they are when she is bathing Joshua or reading him a story, or like she said, when she is nursing Maria. Motherhood gave Sarah such joy and fulfilment, but, in my ignorance, it had never occurred to me that once a woman marries and has children, she would want to do anything else but attend to her husband and children's needs. The role of carer seemed apparent while the man did the hunter-gatherer role.

Jesus was watching my reaction and he smiled at me as if he could read my thoughts - which he probably could, "Simon Peter, what do you think of that? Sarah has found joy and passion for something other than her current role as a wife and a mother. Are you willing to give her the opportunity to do both, after all, she bore and fed your two children?" He smiled as he knew I would not argue. I nodded and embraced Sarah to say how proud I was of her and how blessed I was to have her as my wife.

From that day on, Sarah spent two days a week in the workshop helping Jesus and making a living too from the wood carvings. On these days I laid nets in the morning, looked after the children and collected the catch when Sarah came home. She was always in such high spirits after working with wood. She valued and appreciated making a contribution to the house and she cherished her days with the children instead of feeling tired by doing mother and housework chores daily.

In today's world this may be normal, but 2,000 years ago the women were to stay at home but this was not so in Jesus' eyes. He could see how balance was needed in both home and work life. He saw men sharing the role of carer and homemaker, contributing to home life as women, fulfilling their joy and purpose outside the house, contributing to their personal development and society as a whole. Sarah felt so fulfilled with her new position and sharing the family role of childcare within the household. Many of the men in the village were not pleased and made no bones about telling me so. When their wives started asking them to take this stance also and share the duties so that they could do something they had a talent for and loved to do, the answers were often, "your role is at home, I did not marry you to have to stay home myself, cook and look after the children, even for a couple of days a week. Speak no more of this woman."

Jesus was saddened by this and he vowed to preach about the importance of sharing and balance between the sexes when he started his ministry work.

Peter's message
Waking up to the God Within

Everyone everywhere can be a rock. They do not have to be attached to any church. This is the truth and has to be told to the world. People are now ready to hear this, regardless of what church leaders and religious institutions think and say. Freedom from the religious institutions is the only way that people can fully become alive and wake up to Source.

How can people be true to themselves? They can wake up and be free by knowing their true essence, the Light within - Source/Spirit/God - but only by delving deeper and coming into this process of being, through their own journey of discovery. By travelling this alone and with God, they come to know God and therefore, know their own true selves.

You have to listen to what I have to say. Failing to do so will only mean that people never wake up. More and more are doing so. It has been written about and spoken by the great mysteries for years. Many suffered and lost their lives because of their mission to tell these words of wisdom. Now is the time for me to speak of this and by doing so, may warn future generations and those reading it today of how critical this is to the survival of the planet earth and all who live on her. Only when every individual wakes up to the God within can the world be saved. It will happen, and my calling to speak now will help reach that mark.

3

Acceptance

I have yet to talk to you of Jesus' love of people, in all that he said and in his actions. I have mentioned his warm smile and how his eyes sparkled and saw right into the soul. When I first met Jesus when we were boys, I knew that there was something very different and special about him. It was a presence like no other when he was within a certain radius, which could be felt so strongly, even if you were far away but had him within your sight. That's what I certainly felt when I first laid eyes on him at the market stalls.

Before he began his ministry and took me and the Apostles with him to spread the word, he had not yet admitted to everyone that he was the Son of God, not because he wanted to deny the fact but that he had not yet been summoned to do so. In the meantime, as I have already stated, he was living the life of a child, of a boy, of a man. During these years of growing up, Jesus was cared for by his mother, Mary and father, Joseph and the Essenes. The Essenes were the community of people whom God had chosen to look after the Holy Family and keep them safe. These people were good and kind and full of Light because they were the loving counterparts who had signed up for this time to be part of Jesus' upbringing and his story. Many of the Essenes are back now on earth, reincarnated to tell this story of how people have to look to the Light/Source/

God within. They were there to witness this over 2,000 years ago and now wish, at this time in history, to reconnect those who wish to with their souls, their true essence - which is God and Christ Consciousness.

I can give many examples of how Jesus connected with the people he met. The Essene community who looked out for him were wary when strangers talked to him as he drew many to him, from all walks of life. On one occasion he was talking to two men who were passing through. He had left his workshop to go and buy some bread for lunch. It was a day that Sarah was with him and he had said he'd get lunch that day. Sarah told me he came back with bread, cheese and two men from another land who were travelling together to see other countries and cultures.

They had been drawn, of course, to talk to Jesus and he asked them to join us for lunch. During the conversations over lunch, they had commented on how great it was to see a woman enjoying her work outside the home, that they had never seen this before, and it was very unusual and would not happen in their country. The men, both artistic and creative, appreciated how important this was, what a gift it was to be passionate about something and then to have the opportunity to do what you loved. The conversation was so stimulating, that the lunch went well into the afternoon and a few hours later the four of them were still talking.

(Do not analyse what I say but open your heart and listen. I have more to tell about the two men that came to have lunch with Jesus and Sarah.)

Because the company was so good, Jesus asked them would they like to stay the night - they could stay in the workshop. Sarah said she would like them to stay for supper and meet me and the children. She told Jesus to tell Mary and his mother to come too. Jesus was excited about the impromptu supper.

What a wonderful evening we had with these interesting characters who loved our children, our home, our food and our company.

After the children were in bed and Mother Mary had gone back home, the six of us sat and talked some more. They talked of how they loved children and had nieces and nephews back home. They hadn't talked of womenfolk, so it was clear they were not married. They told us they had to leave their homeland because of their friendship and not choosing to marry and take wives of their own.

I can say honestly and categorically now, as this is scribed, Jesus said to them "do you love like man and wife?" They both replied "we do" and the older one said "we have never voiced this to anyone before, but we trust you all not to judge us."

Jesus asked them to both stand up, they did. He took them both by the hand and asked them to take each other's hands, so the three of them stood in a circle. "I tell you now," he said, "and I am not preaching this from the rooftops yet, as I am still living life normally before my ministry, but I am the Son of God. And, as the Son of God, I can tell you, my Father does not judge. He loves you both. You love each other, yes?" They both nodded. "So be it," he replied, "yes, we need men and women to be together to procreate but not everyone wants to do this and there are enough in the world to do so. So those who choose to be with the same gender to love, this is blessed by God, as love is love."

This was a revelation to all of us. Such a subject was never spoken about and deemed to be a sin - so we were told by our elders - in the eyes of God. Yet here was God's only begotten son, telling us that this was not a sin. Why would it be? If it's love - that love is love - why make laws about who we love? Not everyone is that way inclined therefore the population will continue, so why would this be an issue. Those who protest too much have indeed not looked at the love in the bigger sense and they must do this to be with Source/Spirit/God.

Our new friends were so humbled and so full of love and relief at Jesus' response. These two Holy Men had carried such guilt about how they felt. As two consenting adults, they knew they both wanted the relationship and could not hide their feelings for each other.

This news will be very controversial in today's world. The twenty first century is so open and accepting in one way yet so closed and disapproving in many others. Those who disapprove of what I have recalled will say it is made up and look to the bible to back up their views. But I tell you now, this is what happened. This is what Jesus said, and I was there. I saw the love and acceptance in his eyes and felt the sincerity in his heart when he took both these men by the hand and gave them both his Father's blessing. Again, there was no disapproval, only love.

On another day Jesus arrived with strangers, a day that he and I were going out fishing. He loved to come with me to assist and just be at sea. He said that being out on the boat made him feel so connected to his Father/Source/God.

Anyway, on that particular day he arrived with a man and a woman, who were what people would now group as Travellers. They were not from our parts and were passing through. They were shabbily dressed and looked tired and hungry and sad.

"Peter, have we room for two more?" he said. I felt annoyed at him. Who were these people? What did they want? And why were they here? I did not want to take them with us.

Firstly, I cherished that time I had alone with Jesus. Being in his energy out at sea was such a wonderful and healing experience, and I did not want to share this with anyone. Secondly, this man and women could be dangerous; they could steal my boat, throw us overboard and take the catch. I didn't trust them.

Jesus could sense my reluctance to welcome this couple, so he whispered to me, "be not afraid Peter, these people are God's people, like me and you. Please welcome them. They may not live like you but that does not make them any less in the eyes of my Father."

As always when he spoke this way, I felt humbled by his words. I smiled at this couple and said, "welcome aboard". I added "you look hungry, would you like some food before we head out on the fishing trip?" They nodded and then devoured the bread and meats I had packed for lunch, so Jesus went to get some more food for us to take out on the boat.

The couple were in their early thirties. They had come from a travelling community and were on their way to join family who had travelled ahead of them. They lived a life of moving from town to town and camping by the roadside. They knew that many townspeople did not welcome or like to have their people about as they felt they were different because they were so unsettled.

Jesus was so interested in their lifestyle. He asked lots of questions about where they had been and how they earned a living, what foods they ate, how long did they stay in one place and many more. He talked and they answered, but I know he sensed a real sadness with this couple and although they were polite and answered, they were not joyful in their being and this was very apparent when they spoke.

When we were out at sea, the nets were cast and we had time to sit and just be. Jesus looked into the woman's eyes and asked, "is your sadness due to your childlessness?" She looked up with tears in her eyes and replied, "yes." Her husband held her hand and said, "our people love to have big families and our many brothers and sisters are filling their tents full of children. We camp next to them and hear the laughter, the crying, the playfulness and we feel the love. Although we receive the love from our many nieces and nephews, we so wish for children of our own. We are in our thirties now and we have been married fifteen years. It has not happened yet. It makes me sad but I love my wife and I can accept this but she is so sad and low about it. I fear she may end her life. That is why we have taken a break from being with the family circle as it is too painful to be around all the children and pregnant woman. Two of her sisters and my sister and niece are with child right now, it's too much for my wife to bear." He took a deep breath and lowered his eyes to the ground again. At this stage his wife was weeping and wailing, the boat shook with emotions coming from her slim body.

Jesus listened attentively to all that was said. He looked with such love to the couple. A couple that townsfolk would shun for their appearance and lifestyle. He asked them both to face him and he took both their hands, making like he did before, a circle of the three of them. His presence alone was enough for the woman to stop crying, her wailing ceased and all was calm. "I tell you now" said Jesus, "you have come with us today and accepted our hospitality and kindness, even though we are not your community and from the settlers who normally do not give you the time of day. You trusted Peter and I, and our friendship. I will also tell you something you do not know, that I am the Son of God and at that moment he looked at the man and woman, "I ask you both can I put my hands on your womb?" They nodded in the hope and belief in the miracle about to occur.

Jesus laid his hands on the traveling women, and her husband put his hands on top of his. For a few minutes they stayed like this. I watched in awe. Then Jesus said, "go now, be like man and wife together over the next few days and in nine months' time your child will be born and she will be the first of many."

The sky had been cloudy, yet all of a sudden, the sun peeked out and shone on them both. The women's whole demeanour changed. All of a sudden, she seemed lighter, the heaviness and sadness that had consumed her was gone. Her eyes sparkled and she smiled for the first time since we had met. Her husband's energy shifted too. He was smiling, hugging his wife and saying, "oh God is good. This is a miracle.

Thank God we listened to the voices that told us to go fishing with the settlers."

Meanwhile Jesus looked up to the sky and beckoned with his hands to include us all as he said, "thank you Source, you are the Light and you make all things well when we believe in you and the miracles. By listening to you, from their voices within, their intuitions, this lovely couple will now be parents and their belief in their souls has made this so.

Peter's Message
Opening Up to Your Light and Your Authentic Self

As I have told you in the last three stories, Jesus had time for everyone. He saw their unique gifts and talents, their relationship preferences and picked up on their personal stories and difficulties in their lives. When on earth, it was his mission, even before he started his ministry, to make sure he was aligning people to their specific life purposes, life loves and life lessons. His encounter with the two men and the travelling couple parallel today's difficulties in the world, where many do not accept same-sex relationships and may feel unaccepting of the ways of travellers and refugees. In Jesus' world, no one is different. We are all one. We all come from the same Source and that Light is in every one of us.

Jesus was so supportive of women and saw their role in making a huge impact on society, if given the chance to do so. Throughout the centuries women's roles have changed. Women have a family and a career, yet with the growth of the material world, both men and women seem to need to work to pay the bills, whereas Jesus saw great balance in both genders sharing the family childcare and household duties, doing with less material things. The simplifying of life is essential right now, not 'work, work, work!' and so busy with children's activities that they don't have time to just be.

Observing Jesus in these years before his ministry officially began was such a blessing. I saw, heard and felt how he yearned for people to open up themselves to trusting in their own inner wisdom, which is of course their Light within, which is their Higher Power/Spirit/Source/God within. By doing so, all is well and as it should be, because when connecting with the Light, nothing matters only the Light and the Light will guide you always. Darkness only comes when we are blocking out the Light but as we all know, there was and always will be Light before dark. Sometimes, many times, the darkness has to come so that you can be in it and feel it, but once you ask Source to help you, so the healing begins.

With many churches still, healing is viewed only as something ordained clergy can do, but this is not so, though unfortunately throughout the years this is what we have been taught to believe. Basically, we can all heal ourselves. We have the power within us, we have just forgotten the tools. Energy healing can be taught and given to us by these healers in the holistic therapies, such as Reiki, but again many churches still tell us this is wrong. Jesus was a healer, he taught others to heal. We all have old wounds to heal, we all have old wounds to break free from and by clearing these we make way for more and more Light so that we can walk, talk, feel lighter and be our true authentic selves. But we can only do this by freeing ourselves from the regulations of religious institutions who give us grief for not obeying their rules.

As Jesus showed me clearly in the years we spent together, every one of us is born awake, aware that we have this Light within. Then we forget and become what our parents, and schools and churches say, or rebel against them and veer away from God. More and more people are coming back to Source. This time of Christ Consciousness is like the Second Coming, though Jesus is not physically appearing, he is sending his messages through those who have come to spread the word in books, workshops, podcasts, social media, and YouTube videos. It's all out there and the energy is changing and it is all perfect. So be it!

4

Unconditional Love

Jesus loved all people, even those who tried to harm him when he was a baby and a boy. He sent them loving prayers and forgiveness.

We were discussing one day, over breakfast, how Herod's guards had searched for him and murdered so many baby boys along the way. He prayed and sent healing to those parents and the families of those who lost their sons, brothers and grandsons. Jesus said, "I forgive them for they know not what they do." I was surprised at this remark. "But Jesus," I said, "how can they not know what they did? Are they not brothers, fathers themselves? How would they feel if guards came and killed their sons or brothers and how could they kill a little innocent baby?"

"Well" replied Jesus, "why does anyone do anything evil or harmful? Out of fear, of course. They were told by Herod that this baby boy would become king and as this was a threat to Herod, he ordered the guards to find and kill this baby. The fear of a new king was bad enough, as Herod would not have portrayed me in a good light. Also, they would not have disobeyed Herod. This would have cost them their own lives. Those with families would not have left them without a father/ provider so these men had no option but to obey their king and carry out his orders, regardless of their moral opinions."

"So," I said, "what happens these men when they pass over and go to God. What will your Father do? Do these men enter into Heaven or do they go to Hell? I would expect it to be Hell, for they have committed murder by killing these baby boys."

"Yes, you would think that, wouldn't you, but I tell you now, they don't go to this *'Hell'* as you call it."

"So, where do they go? I asked.

"Well, many will repent before they pass over. They will watch their own sons and daughters having sons and in becoming grandfathers and holding in their arms their new born grandsons. In that moment they will remember what they did and they will weep with shame and remorse. In that very moment they will beg God for his forgiveness and by doing so, it will be granted."

I replied "just like that?" "God will forgive the cries of men who murdered innocent children!"

"Yes," Jesus replied, "because that is what unconditional love is. On the realisation of doing this horrendous deed and feeling the shame and sorrow, something has transformed within their being. They have connected to God again, their own Light within, and by doing so, they have come home."

Peter's Message
The False Self, Suicide and Suicide Bombers

God's/Source's/Spirit's unconditional love for us is something that the Bible, and thus religious institutions, do not give a clear message on. Yes, we have a consciousness or conscience that tells us right from wrong and guides us as to how we are to live our lives, especially when we are connected to the Light/God within. In being connected fully we can live a life of Higher Consciousness. Be fully aware of the signs and synchronicities, recognising when the ego comes in which disconnects us from our authentic selves - the one connected to Spirit.

The forces of the ego, the false self, are what makes people hate, lie, cheat, steal, murder and harm themselves and others. It is the false self - the ego - that drives those in such pain in their lifetime to see no other way but ending their lives. The churches, of course, see these all as sins, as are listed in the Ten Commandments. However, I tell you now as I heard Jesus say and know God to do, no one - I repeat - no one is turned away from God's love. He does not forsake anyone. Even the most hunted of villains are accepted with unconditional love.

This may seem absurd, especially in today's world when so many genocides are still going on and refugees are fleeing from their homes. This is when we all get to show our Godliness by helping and accepting these refugees into our countries and giving them shelter. Those who persecuted them, will have their own conscience that will meet God and be greeted by such unconditional love. This love will create a next lifetime of an awakened soul who will come to earth to spread kindness, love and wellbeing. What would punishment serve the soul, only more resentment and hate; that is why God is all about unconditional love.

Yet the churches have had to extend control, which explains why they created the illusions that God is fearful and judgemental to the point of expulsion to the fires of hell. I tell you now, this is not so. Each person who passes over, their souls are greeted by Light and they are surrounded by this unconditional love; love so pure that they will come again to feel it on this earth, to be it and spread this love. Awakened souls on this earth have lived many life times and one of these will have been a life of terror and pain, to come back now to teach of love.

To continue with this subject of taking one's own life, it is now preached by certain extremists that is an honourable thing to do, especially in defence of their faith. Ego-driven males make promises to younger males, vulnerable and open to corruption, that they will be met in the afterlife and greeted by a group of virgins to rejoice their deed. Such false stories are of the ego-mind, and manipulation is behind every one of them. To those suicide bombers who kill others for their own selfish reasons, in the name of God, are totally mistaken and misguided. God greets them, again unconditionally and they repent for what they have done. Their souls return to feel the pain they have caused and then in sorrow return to the Light within or they will return to teach only of love. All is not lost - even the most horrendous of deeds - as God's Light is within each and every one of us.

When the time is right, truth and integrity will come.

It is only when humans have lost their way and blocked out their own inner Light does the darkness of the ego, the false self, get in.

In his teachings, Jesus always spoke of the father's love for his children. We know how to feel this, as parents, so we only have to tune into the love for our own children, no matter what they do - it's unconditional love. This gives a clear example of how we can measure God's/Spirit's/Source's love for all of humanity.

5

Children

Jesus loved children and here I'll tell you his thoughts, feelings and actions I witnessed when he was in the company of children.

As our friendship grew, he would spend more and more time with Sarah and I, and our children, Joshua and Maria. It was a delight to watch him with them. He loved to listen to Joshua's stories, watch him play with his toys and join his make-believe games. He would hold and cuddle Maria as a baby, and help change her and bath her, a role only women did in those days.

His time spent with us as a family was very special indeed. He told us one evening, after supper and when the children were in bed, that he and Mary Magdalene would love a family but that it was not meant to be as his Father had other plans for him. When I asked what the plans were, he replied, "all will be revealed in good time Simon Peter. For now, and before we start my ministry, let us enjoy our time with family and friends, cherishing every moment we can."

One evening by the fire, Joshua was drawing a picture, and Jesus was helping him. Mary was cuddling Maria, and Sarah and I were enjoying their company and this special time together. We knew it would not last forever, as Jesus had told us that we would be travelling when we started the ministry - thus away from home - so these moments were precious.

On that certain evening, a cousin of Sarah's arrived at the door with her daughter, who was about 16 and in tears. Sarah ran to her cousin and asked "what was wrong - was her husband alright? How was her mother?" Sarah was becoming upset too.

"They are all fine," replied her cousin, "It is not them I come about, it is her," as she pointed to the crying girl - "she has disgraced us all."

Sarah put her arm around the sobbing girl and said, "I'm sure it's not that bad?"

The girl could not speak, she was so distressed. The energy between them was very tense and there was such sadness coming from the girl.

"What could possibly be this bad?" said Sarah.

"Well" replied her cousin, "she has told us this evening that she is having a baby next month. She hid it well from us. We will be the talk of the village and disgraced as a family."

This is when Jesus, who had been on the floor with Joshua, stood up and went over to the girl. He put his arms around her, embraced her and said, "congratulations, dear one, you are very blessed to be carrying one of God's children. I tell you now, you have made him happy by giving this new soul life."

The girl stopped crying, in shock at what he had said. She looked at him through her tearstained eyes, smiled and said, "thank you, I feel truly blessed. I was just scared to tell anyone as I know it is seen as a sin by the elders, villagers and my parents, as I am not married. I have been so confused as I feel so connected already to my baby, but I am afraid my parents will make me give my child away to a couple who may be childless and wish for children. I don't want this, I want to keep my baby, no matter what anyone thinks or says." She sighed and sat down in the nearby chair. She was emotionally exhausted.

Meanwhile her mother, who was also emotionally exhausted, sat down on the other chair. She had calmed down and for the first time since they entered our house, she looked at her own child with empathy and love. She took her daughter's hand and said, "I'm sorry, I was thinking only of myself and how others would think of me and your father. I was so wrapped up in me that I forgot about you.

Jesus, I have met you before with Peter and Sarah and I know you are a Holy Man. I trust what you have said is true and I ask my daughter for forgiveness in how I have acted. Like God loves us, I love my daughter and my soon-to-be grandchild too. I feel very blessed and I thank you for making me aware of this."

Jesus walked over and put his arms around them both. He then - like before - took a hand each in his, they took each other's hands too, and the three of them stood in a circle and prayed.

Jesus lead the prayer, thanking the women for bearing God's children and saying how marriage, or no marriage, hadn't any bearing on how much God loved this new baby that would arrive. The matter was irrelevant in God's eyes. Sarah's cousin and her daughter stayed on for late supper and there was much excitement about discussing names for the new arrival.

Jesus smiled and said, "no one is cast aside or put down in God's eyes, those are man-made rules, and people's egos have to get past this fact. God teaches only of unconditional love. All are included. God loves every one of the children who arrived on earth. He does not have a score card for the circumstances in which they arrived; man made that up, as he did so many things.

Jesus loved little children, all children. His eyes would sparkle when Joshua would run and jump into his arms or when Maria laughed with glee when she saw him. He was always gentle and kind with everyone but there was an extra glow about him when he was in the company of children.

I asked him one day, "Jesus, why do children bring out the extra glow in you? What is it about being in their company that holds that special connection?"

"Peter", he replied, "children are the closest bond I have to my Father, as they are full of the Light and love. Little children are so innocent and pure - they still hold the *'I Am Presence'* that humans are all born with but tend to lose bit by bit, the concentrated process of it, as they grow. By the time a child has reached 12 years of age, limited beliefs and patterns - learned through parents, schools, and societies - have formed. You watch little children Peter, they are full of love and they believe they can do anything. They are kind, generous and forgiving.

As they grow some will forget these traits and thus forget about God. They may attend service on the Sabbath and profess to love and honour God. However, if they are not doing this to themselves - love, kindness, generosity & forgiveness - nor to others, how, I ask, can they be close to God? This is hypocritical and they might as well not serve God at all once a week if they cannot do it every day. It is the everyday commitment to be loving oneself, thus loving the God within, that is of the upmost importance to live an enlightened life. In fact, it is vital. And just look at how little children trust their parents. Joshua and Maria trust you will love, feed, clothe them, plus play with them and give them your attention. What happens with adults is that they forget to trust God, Source/Spirit/the Higher Power/Self and look to other ways of gaining what they feel is important, such as money, success, or material things.

They try to control others, manipulate, cheat or even kill if necessary to get what they want and the irony is they have it within all along. Yet people forget. They forget and it is so simple. All they have to do is be still and listen. God, our Higher

Self, guides us all through life but we need to take that time to listen.

This is why I have come here. This is why God sent me. I am here to remind people that God is loving and kind and generous and forgiving. He is not a God of rules, wrath, control, and punishment. He has the gentleness and kindness of a little child and he is filled with unconditional love. Those who come back to him will be blessed with insights and messages of how to journey through life on this path of love. Because that is all that matters in any lifetime, that one's journey is filled with love - love for self, others, nature, the environment. And of course, by doing this, one is walking hand in hand with God my Father."

Peter's Message
Simple Rules of Living on this Earth

We are called - called by God - to serve ourselves as if we are Him/Her. Jesus showed this while he was on earth. He showed us all how this unconditional love is the only way to live and he used little children as an example of how to be — loving, kind, gentle, forgiving. By spending these thirty-three years on earth, Jesus got to experience all emotions and be on the receiving end of both feelings and actions, being the polar opposite of unconditional love.

In today's world we see the pain and suffering that still exists, the famine and hunger in some parts of the world and the grandiosity and extreme wealth in others. This saddens us looking on and is even summarised in the Black Eyes Peas song 'Where is the love?'

While not everyone has forgotten about Jesus' words and his teachings, those who have will have to rise up and remember. This will be done in both loud and discrete ways as other Light-workers make their marks on society, which can assist the change in hearts, minds and souls.

Have compassion for those who are not yet ready to live here in the Light, they will one day live a life of love.

In the meantime, be gentle with yourselves. Live simply. Be grateful for everything (even the hardships). Be kind. Spend time in nature. Don't judge others or yourself. Listen to your intuition. Live purposefully and most of all, LOVE, LOVE, LOVE.

Daily Silence

Jesus loved to be around people but he also loved to be alone, in silence. He would take himself off to be quiet and in doing so talk to God. I was intrigued at why he needed to do this at least twice a day and asked him to share with me so that I to could go to that place he called 'peace.'

"Peter," he said, "life is busy. People are working, looking after families, playing, and in all that is going on many forget that there is a God within every one of them and that God has to be honoured by them daily. By doing this ritual of taking time out to be alone with themselves, they can go deeper, reflect and clear any thoughts and emotions that do not serve them. Also, and most importantly, they can listen to that voice within, the inner voice that guides them throughout their lives. It is by listening to God/Source/Spirit/their Higher Power that they become whole and receive the messages that guide them to their true calling, their life purpose on their journey through this lifetime."

"So, how do I do this Jesus?" I asked, "I am familiar with prayers at the temple, but that is in large groups. Do I really need to be alone?" "Most definitely!" he replied, "it is the space between the breaths that connects us to God and by doing so we can truly be in the 'I Am Presence.' Because Peter, you have to remember, you are a Spark of the Divine, therefore you too are God."

"But Jesus" I asked, "is that not blasphemy? How can I be like God? I am not worthy. Have I not sinned? I am not free from sins, I know that."

"Peter, of course you are worthy, everyone on earth is. They were created in the image of God. It is as simple as that. It is only when people forget where they come from, that they lose their connection with God and therefore themselves. How many people do you know who are obsessed with making money, climbing social ladders and buying things they do not need?

It's a way of life to many - doing, buying, saying things that are not necessary. God wishes us to live life simply, and the most important thing we can do is be love, give love and, of course, the main component here is to love ourselves. By doing so, we love the God within, which is God. And also, when we spend time with God, we listen to the messages that will guide us and take us on our life purpose, where we find joy and spread this joy, as we are so fulfilled and full of love. And again, it is back to taking time to be silent, to be alone, to be."

What if people don't get the chance to be alone? What if they are busy with work and then have families?" I said. "There are no excuses," Jesus replied, "everyone can find even five minutes at the beginning and end of the day to be alone, or even in the middle of the day. People have to make an effort, be away from all distraction and sit in silence. Once they do this for a few days it becomes a ritual they look forward to. After a few weeks they have built this time into their day.

Being in nature is very calming and a good place to go to just be. Listening to the birds, watching the water ripple, looking at the trees sway in the whistling wind. These are all aspects of God's creations. The God that is in every one of us, is that little bird, the tree, the lake. When people really realise this amazing resource in wonder and in awe, they will feel closer and closer to God. By respecting and loving the environment around us, we are honouring what God gives us here on earth, this place, that for now, we call home."

"But," I asked, "how do we do this Jesus? How do we teach people to be in silence, spend time alone?" He replied, "we just keep doing it Peter and people will talk about it. You can plant the seeds with your fishermen friends. How many times have you been out on the boat, sat in silence, enjoyed the peace and tranquillity, and appreciated the beauty of the sun shining on your face, the water lapping up on the boat, the blue sky, clear glass calm seas and a mild wind on your face? You may have sighed, connecting with yourself and nature, and then being at one with God within, therefore God.

Many seem to be under the impression that they have to be seen to be with God. That if they pray weekly with others, then that ticks a box and they will be ok until the next week, despite the fact they may do ungodly acts in the six days in between. To be seen to be with God for the fear of God's so-called wrath, or what people might think if you did not go to worship, or to show you attend to be seen to be Godlike, are no reasons that are aligned to God and the love that he has.

My Father does not demand you to be seen in a public place to be with Him. You can connect in your kitchen, out fishing, on a walk, anywhere and everywhere as long as you have time to be in silence, in moments of retreat from the outside world."

"But what about the elders?" I asked, "they demand it, as it is sinful if we do not attend and pay our dues to the temple. And does it not say to obey the Sabbath and worship God?"

"Peter, I tell you now, no one has to listen to anyone else's rules about when or where they spend time with God. Everyone has their own special and unique relationship with God and it is personal - not anyone else's business. Therefore, if someone connects in with God daily, in silence, why would they need to go and publicly pray? They can if they wish, but there is no need. Their relationship with God is already solid and true, and they are following the guidance from within. This is God. God speaks to them daily and in the silence sends messages which leads them to spreading joy, and most importantly, love.

Those who attend on the Sabbath because of fear or the need to be seen, they do not attend from a place of love."

"So, what you are saying is: daily practice is much more powerful that a weekly hour with God!" I said.

"Correct Peter, my Father would rather hear the voice daily of the man who has never entered a temple door, rather than the man who does not connect when he is in there and spend the rest of the week speaking of people, cheating, lying and generally not being loving and connected to God. If the relationship is not made with the God within in silence, how can people expect to attend on the Sabbath and continue a relationship that has never been nurtured. This makes no sense at all."

"Thank you, Jesus, this all makes sense to me now. I have been connecting all along while out fishing, I am more aware now of how to really tune into and be with God.

Jesus replied, "that's great Peter, now let us eat and enjoy some time with the children. We'll tell them how important it is to be silent and spend time alone. This is a vital tool for parents to teach and show their offspring."

Peter's Message
Slow Down, Be Still and Listen to the God Within

Jesus clearly tells of the importance of just being, being silent, to be with God. In today's world we look on from the Higher Dimensions, which you may call heaven, and see a society that is filled with so many distractions which nearly makes it's impossible to 'just be.' Only those who are aware, or feel overwhelmed by today's busy world, take time to be still. Being still is what makes you grow, grow spiritually, grow personally, grow closer to God and thus be your authentic self. Anything outside of that is an illusion, of no relevance to the home you came from, and to the place you will return.

Yes, today's technology - the world wide web, social media, fitness gadgets, and constant gaming, and having everything instantaneously - in the rapidly developing world are all alright in moderation, but what we can see and feel is the constant need for these items, these programmes, these sites.

We ask you why? Why? Why? What would happen tomorrow if the worldwide web crashed? If you didn't have your social media to browse twenty times a day? Your Sky TV to pause while you make tea? Your wrist band to connect your steps? Your games that keep you up all night? If they all disappeared tomorrow would you feel devastated, empty, alone? What would you do? It's that simple.

The amazing thing is, you'd still be you. You may not have all your gadgets and attachments and technology to know what everyone else is doing, so you'd have to be alone with yourself, with you, with God.

How does that make you feel? Is it terrifying? Could you do it? If you feel you could, then you have enough awareness and connections with self and God to keep going on your journey with full support from all in the Higher Realms.

If not, then you need to STOP, you need to look at where you are in your life, and reassess how attached you are in your life, and re-evaluate how attuned you are to all these man-made devices outside of yourself. Yes, they are needed for vital information, for promoting business, for keeping in touch - BUT - it's when they take over your lives, that you become disconnected.

When something on Facebook keeps you from sleeping, or something that someone didn't say or share on it has you consumed by your thoughts, that's when you know it's time to take a break and come back to God. And by coming back, you feel yourself again, the true you, the authentic you, the you that you truly know, remember and love.

Many of you will come back, and many won't. But that's ok too. You may return in another incarnation and on a next life you will choose to be quiet and be silent, live simply and humbly and be close to God.

We ask people to look at how the indigenous people live and lived. The native American Indians, the Maori, the Inuit - they all lived so connected to nature, and therefore close to God. Their traditions have carried on, and although the world has caught up, these people still have elders passing on their grounded ceremonies and way of life that keep them so connected to Spirit.

We see you struggling at this earthly time to make sense of it all. So much has changed over the past decade that makes life so fast. Everyone is so busy. It's as if life gives you no other choice. It's as if you all think there is no other way, this is the way, busy, busy, busy and you tell everyone 'I'm busy, busy, busy!' Then when you have slowed down, be present to just slowing down, and be, just be.

We can't stress enough again the need to slow down this pace of life you are living. What kind of existence is this for children who are now programmed for instant gratification, constant gadgets in their hands, going to bed with them in their laps? What happened to a bedtime story and night-time prayers? What kind of hope does that give to the next generation? How can they ever learn the importance of silence, going within and spending time with God if it is not taught at home, if it is not shown as the way to be? How will children make choices by being their authentic selves if they do not even know how to be?

I tell you now that Jesus taught me about silence. He taught the Apostles too: he told us, 'Be still and know that I Am God' yet the world is still not listening. Yes, mindfulness is now scientifically proven to help with stress and promote brain function, and the list goes on BUT mindfulness is not enough. People still need to connect in to that still place inside. The world must wake up to this now - do this, be this, just be and be with God.

This time of quiet contemplation can be done alone in mediation, or if preferred, in a group setting. Meditation groups are excellent and learning new meditation practices are ways to connect with the God within. The more people who come back to this way of being with Spirit - rather than listening to men preach of hell, fire and brimstone - the better the world will be. Those who preach of hell and scare their congregations are living in total fear themselves.

The illusion by the congregation that these men know this to be truth, or that he is better than them because he has studied the religion of the bible, is ridiculous and absurd. No one, I repeat no one, is superior or inferior to anyone in the eyes of God. As many of the new age spiritual practices tell you, we are all One, all connected - All living within all people, animals, nature.

Just because someone has studied – yes, they might have extra knowledge on the subject - but when it comes to God, no one knows the depth of His love and commitment to the children other than Him and His love that is in everyone.

Again, people have forgotten. Therefore, they do not connect, and they feel that those above them in churches, those ordained, those who speak of God are more Godly than they are. I tell you now, this is not so.

Life Purpose

In the times of Jesus, it was common for adult children to live with their parents and grandparents and bring up their own children in such expanded family circles. People lived by the ways of their people, their upbringing was passed on to their children, and their children's children and so on, and the generations carried on these traditions. Their ways became law because their elders, years ago, said so. Jesus was all for old traditions if the values matched what he felt came from God/Source/Spirit, otherwise he challenged these traditions and was all for change.

One day as we left his workshop we met a man chastising his son, "why can't you work hard like I do? Your grandfather and your great grandfather set up this business, they will be turning in their tombs right now. You are a disgrace to this family."

The young man who was about 18 was both angry and sad. "Why Papa? Why make me do the work when I don't like it? Give the business to my sister, she loves this work and has a flair for it. Don't I tell you, I hate it, I want to paint."

The father roared, "leave this business and you are dead to me. What kind of nonsense is that, a woman cannot take over this business when I am gone, no matter how good she is at it. Plus, her place will be at home when she marries and has children." And at that he stormed off.

The young man hung his head and turned to go towards the sea.

Jesus stopped him. "Do you mind me saying something?" "No, not at all," he replied." "You probably tell me that you are agreeing with my father." "Well, I'm not agreeing," Jesus replied, "though I can see his hurt and disappointment, but that does not make it right."

"So, what is right then?" the young man asked. "I do not want to be a book-keeper and accountant. I hate it - it bores me and I find it difficult. I want to do what I love, but if I do that my father will forsake me, I could not bear that."

"But you are willing to sell out to do something you hate, how will that feed your soul?" asked Jesus. "It won't, but it's the sacrifice I will have to make," he replied. "Oh!" said Jesus, "a martyr in the making, good luck!"

"What do you mean good luck?" The young man asked. "I mean what I say,' replied Jesus, "good luck with spending the rest of your life denying your soul's calling and staying for the sake of duty."

"But what am I to do?" he asked. My father is a stern man and has no time for what he calls my foolish ideas." "You are a young man," Jesus replies, "and you have this opportunity now to step up and follow your heart, your soul's calling. You sister is interested in the business; you must talk to her, come up with a viable plan and present this to your father. Give him options. Tell him if this idea does not work out then you will return to the family business within three years."

"Do you think he'll go for this?" asked the young man. "My father is a very stubborn man and does not like to be challenged. His word is law in our family. He does not back down or change his mind."

"Then use your creative gifts to show him how serious you are," Jesus suggested. "Paint him a magnificent picture by putting all your love for painting and for your father into it, regardless of the outcome. By doing so, with no attachment, your soul will guide you. I can tell you now, if you do this, your father will see what lights you up and he will grant you this absence, to be who you want to be, in this lifetime. And, in time, your sister may marry a man who has the same love for accounting as your father, which will be perfect, and free your sister to have a family and be part of the business too."

"Oh, that would be indeed be ideal," he smiled. "My father would have the son he always wanted!" "No!" replied Jesus, "do not say that. He will have a son-in-law that he will love and appreciate, but do not think that he never wanted you because you are different to him."

"But I do feel that at times," stated the young man, "and many times growing up, I feel my father does not understand me because I am creative and carefree, and we clash because I have no time for his dominant ways and his obsession to make money."

"This is common," replied Jesus. "Many parents and their children have very different attitudes to life but underneath it all you must understand - that no matter what your father says or how he treats you - he does love you unconditionally. Even though he may not show it. Deep in his soul, he chose you to be his son, to challenge him and broaden his horizons to give him the opportunity to look at things differently."

The young man exclaimed, "oh, I never thought of it like that before. I guess I feel he would like a son like my friend Paul, who is willingly going to work with his father. It just makes things so easy and uncomplicated."

"But,' said Jesus, "look at the lessons both you and your father are learning here. If he had been supportive of you from the beginning, you would not have gained the skills of negotiation and explaining your cause. Plus, it proves how passionate you are about painting, when you are going to paint for him and prove how much it means to you. Also, your sister will thank you."

"Jesus," the young man said, "I heard you were a Holy Man but I did not believe it until now. You have soul wisdom and I can hear your support for me and the empathy for my father. My father is but a creation of his own upbringing, which was one of following his own father's footsteps, working hard and making money to support his family and to give him status in the community. I thank you for taking the time to talk to me. You were just passing by and overheard our conversation. I am glad you were passing at the time."

Jesus smiled, "I was just passing, as this has been planned by God, my Father - your Heavenly Father - who wants you to break free and love your life's purpose. When you were born, God knew you would meet me today and have this conversation. It is all perfect and as it is meant to be. Now go and speak with your sister and prepare your painting with love. I look forward to meeting you again, James, when you are living and doing what you came to earth to do - be an artist."

Peter's Message
Unhappy? – Then follow Your Soul's Calling

Being with Jesus this day and now recalling the conversation through my scribe, God and Jesus want people to know the importance of tapping into one's own true-life purpose. Everyone comes to earth to learn lessons, love and evolve, and every person carries with them their own unique talents. When utilised, these talents are spectacular and those who use them will shine. Their talents will always be used for the greatest good, otherwise they are wasted. All life purpose comes from a place of love.

What happens to many though is that they listen to parents and teachers or go for careers because of money or necessity; they think logically instead of coming from their heart and soul. If only people looked and listened and felt the joy in the activities that bring them peace. The sense of bliss, where they feel right at home - as if they could do this forever - that's where they find God/Source/Spirit, that's what it is like to be evolved and in higher vibration, in another dimension, that is where all people find true love.

This true and everlasting love is within them, in the bliss, peace, joy, excitement, happiness that they feel. That's God's Presence, the 'I Am Presence,' that's what one's true calling is all about - coming *home to oneself - doing and sharing the activities that fulfil them and feeds their soul.*

So why? Oh, why do so many still strive to spend most of their lives doing jobs, courses, climbing up career ladders, involved in activities they either dislike, despise or even hate? Is this not insane? No wonder there are so many unhappy people in the world on antidepressants because they are so unfulfilled. If only they could tap into their soul's calling, then the medical companies would be able to pour their research into other treatments.

What is needed for this vicious circle to stop? – of children going to school, leaving and getting a meaningless job or training course in which they have no interest. Or going to college or university and completing a course they do not have a passion for. Those who are lucky enough to find what they love, early on in life, flourish. They are, as Sir Ken Robinson says, 'in their element' and so be it; they are fulfilling what they came on earth to do, to shine, shine, shine!

Although these people who do follow their passion, many of them may not believe in God. So, they will find this statement absurd, but I can tell you now 'they are close to God.' They are actually closer in vibrational harmony than an ordained priest or clergy man who went into church service because it was expected of them by parents or teachers, or they were pushed into it due to family tradition. If someone, no matter who they are, what or where they are, spends a lifetime in their working years doing something they do not like and it turned into hatred, then they are denying their souls, and therefore themselves, so much joy, bliss, peace and love.

They only way to follow your life purpose is to listen to the calling, look out for the signs, feel what feels right, and knowing it is so. And to truly find it, quiet meditation and connecting with God/Source/Spirit will lead you there, if you have not found it already.

There are those who have found the treasure and the irony is that everyone has the same treasure. The only thing is that so many are not prepared to dig deep enough to find it and pay attention to their intuitive ability and let the ego dissolve, so as not to care about money, status and material things.

Jesus had neither time for such worldly possessions nor man's fight to gain more and more, doing what they despised to earn it. He saw the need for food, shelter and goods and he knew that comfort made life easier to bear, but he saw no pleasure in greed and status. When doing what you came here to do - in doing your life's purpose and in following your soul's calling - abundance will come because it is your right. You will be rewarded for seeking, listening for and feeling that which makes your soul sing. In so doing, you are doing what God sent you on earth to do, in your own unique way.

Shine, shine, shine! And by doing so, contribute to society and spread love and joy to others. This can be done in many ways — teaching, baking, healing, sewing, farming, inventing, writing, whatever - but just do it, and evolve. Jesus spoke of this often. It is what God wants all on earth to do, to be whole and at one with themselves, with each other and ultimately one with God.

8

All Living Things

When Jesus was around animals and birds, one could not help but notice how they reacted when he was near. There was a sense of calmness and a serene feeling of oneness.

One day in the market, a bull got free from a pen and it went wild chasing through the stalls with people screaming. Mothers were pulling their children close, fathers and boys were reaching for sticks and rocks to be used as weapons and babies cried out, picking up on the fear of their parents and the crowd. "Get out of the way," I shouted at Jesus, as the raging bull came running towards us. I was terrified, yet Jesus stood still, raised his arms out, as if to greet the bull.

"No" shouted, the owner of this animal, "he is fierce, move quickly, he will kill you!"

Jesus stood on where he was, calm and trusting the process. Once the bull was almost upon him, it stopped. We all - me, the owner, and the crowds in the market - looked on in amazement as Jesus reached out and hugged this ferocious bull. The bull, got down on his knees and put his large head, with big horns, on Jesus lap. He then rolled over for Jesus to tickle his tummy. It was the most bizarre sight any of us had ever seen.

The owner was so shocked he had to sit down.

"That is the scariest bull I have ever owned," he said. "That's why I brought it to market today. Look at it now? What magic powers do you have Jesus?"

Jesus smiled and answered, "I only have within what you all possess, but have forgotten." The man replied, "you mean, I could do that, stop a raging a bull and have it be gentle towards me? I don't think so. I have never, in all my life as a farmer and working with animals, witnessed such a thing. Even the most experienced of animal handlers could not do what you have just done."

"Well", Jesus said, "I tell you now, anyone who comes to know God in such a way that they become His very Essence - of which everyone is - can relate to animals as I do. Animals too, as are plants, and all living things, are made from the Divine Spark, the Essence of Source, and thus, by respecting them, in the same way as God does, we can connect with them too. Every man and woman can embody this way of being when they realise they are equal to everyone else – that their connection to the Divine is no greater or lesser than any other person as everyone is the same, because we are all One.

"But that is ok you saying that," the farmer said, "do I just realise this truly and then I can do what you did?"

"What I did was exceptional because I am on a higher vibration," said Jesus, "but everyone can move higher and they can only do this by clearing old baggage and limiting beliefs and bringing their energy in alignment to Source."

"What else do we have to do?" asked the farmer. "Talk to God, Jesus replied, "in the silence of meditation, eat good wholesome food, drink plenty of water, exercise, be gentle, be kind and most of all love. Love everyone and everything. Love is all that matters to God/Spirit/Source. By being love, you are in direct alignment to your Higher Self which is Spirit/Source/God. Young children and animals are already so connected. It comes naturally to them so they can feel and sense true alignment of others. Have you ever had a dog bark at someone who is being nice to you, but later you find they were not a very nice person and tried to double cross you?"

"Yes!" said the farmer. "Only last week, a man who wanted to sell me some sheep, he was so pleasant, I bought them and found out a few days later they were full of disease and they died days later. Our farm dog had snarled and barked the entire visit."

"Do you see? asked Jesus, "the dog picked up on his energy, but you were fooled by his charms. We can learn so much from animals and we must give them the respect and love that they deserve. Anyone who is cruel to them is not living in alignment to Source, for God sees no joy in anything that is deemed cruel to any living creature in the world."

Jesus and I left the market, with the farmer in awe of Jesus' words and he changed his mind about selling this bull, who was like a little lamb by the time we left, with children coming over to pet him in his pen.

As we walked home by the sea, I was more observant of how creatures were around him. Birds would come close, sometimes hopping on his shoulders. Dogs and cats would come to be stroked. As we passed a field, donkeys neighed and trotted to the gate to be petted. "You really do, have a way with animals and birds!" I said. "I noticed it before, but really seeing it now, it's amazing."

"It is only what we all have inside of us," added Jesus," that connection to Source, which these animal and birds share with us. They connect with the Sameness, they are connecting with the love."

"Love? but do animals know how to love?" I asked.

"Just look at that ewe with her new born lambs, a cat with her kittens, a bird feeding her nest of chicks, if that's not love, what is? Instinct, survival, duty, the laws of nature, yes, but the basis of it all is connection, protection and love."

Peter's Message
Love & Respect Nature, and All Living Things

What I want to convey here is the message of love and respect for all living things. Man has hunted for survival for food to feed his family, since time began. In those days, people respected the animals and gave thanks for them before the hunt and in what they provided for their survival. Times changed, animals have been treated badly and used in sport for the satisfaction of greedy men. Killing for the fun of it. This is not how God envisaged animals would be used, or how they would live. Kindness means kindness and that is of upmost importance, even more so, if animals are used in the food chain.

Today, we watch as the environment is also treated with disrespect in many parts of the world. We see how the oceans and rivers are being polluted, how waste from industries is sadly disposed of, and how chemicals are dispersed out into the air that is meant to be clean and pure. We do see that governments are making an effort now to keep the environment in good shape, but worldwide not all governments are doing this, so it is not enough. Many animals, birds and fish will become extinct and this is not what God wants.

Jesus was so aware of the world when he was on earth. He saw the need for clean water, fresh air, beautiful nature, healthy animals and crops, plentiful fish and birds singing in the sky. His love for nature, all living things and the environment spoke volumes for where the world needs to be right now. Why would God/Source/ Spirit give us these wonderful creatures and resources for us to treat them disrespectfully and harm them? That would make absolutely no sense at all. God asks you to treat your world with love. Be kind and loving to all living creatures and the environment, including being mindful to create a healthy food chain in farming methods. Let no cruelty to animals exist, as they too feel pain and deserve to be treated equally, in the same way as you would like to be treated yourself. This may seem absurd, but it is not. Why would it be? All living things have the same Source energy as you. Respect is essential. Kindness and respect for all who come from Universal energy is what lights up the world and makes it grow and grow.

Those who do not eat meat will feel lighter. God does not condemn those who do. He condemns no one but being meat-free is healthier for the body and more favourable to the soul. Those who do eat meat must thank the animal before doing so. This officially respects its time here on earth and its purpose to live fully, and when its existence ends, it helps feed and nourish you.

Fish are plentiful in the oceans and as long as they are not over-fished, are nourishing food. They have been free until their time to feed the soul.

Plants and vegetables grow with many nutrients to keep human bodies healthy and strong. The importance of production in organic ways is essential.

Lastly, in this message, the trees - treasure the trees. They are old and wise and they flow with life through the changing seasons. They are grounded and steadfast and tall. Hugging a tree is not 'fluffy.' Jesus did this many times, he had the Apostles doing it too. He told us all, "by doing this act, you are closest to God."

Thomas had protested! "How can we be closest to God by hugging a tree?" Are we not closest when we are on our knees praying!" "No!" replied Jesus. "This act of connecting with the tree, feeling its trunk, pressing your face on the bark, that is God you are close to. It's God's/Source's/Spirit's energy in the tree, the same energy that is in you. Feel the energy and look at how its roots are down in the earth. Yet it stands tall and reaching up to the sky, proud to be a tree and going with the flow of growing shoots and leaves in spring, blooming for summer and showing colour and foliage leaves turning brown and red and yellow in autumn and falling off, and then bare in winter and so the cycle repeats.

God is in charge here and the trees respond and accept. He loves and protects the birds who nest everywhere - in tree houses, in gardens or in the forest. I tell you all now to hug trees. They are Divine. Connect, connect with God.

Alone & Gathering

In my time with Jesus, he talked a lot about time alone with God and he talked and demonstrated the importance of being with people who were on their path too. He said that when people gathered and talked the same language in relation to love of Source, themselves and others, this way of being together was rejoiced by God. So, spend such time together, spread the good vibes and energy, and thus connect more and more people to become awakened to their own Light/Source/God.

One day Jesus met me after I came off the boat. He asked me and a few of the other fishermen would we like to gather for some supper, and to bring our wives and children too. It was the loveliest impromptu evening, one which we all cherished. While he and Mary cooked, his mother Mary chatted with our wives, and the children all played happily. It was blissful indeed. And during supper Jesus would ask questions to initiate discussion. He was so good at including everyone - the children too. He would ask questions, "when was the last time you felt true kindness towards yourself?" and "what are you most thankful for, what do you most love to do?" and "what's your passion?"

It was so interesting hearing everyone's replies and the children especially had such lovely answers. So pure and innocent and full of love.

"Look!" said Jesus, "look at how happy everyone is. You are smiling! And you are all listening to each other too! But most of all, it is positive, it is high, it is full of good energy and love. We are gathered together thinking, talking and feeling memories that are love and light. Thus, we stay in the same vibration.

The *'now'* becomes the good vibration and the good vibration in the present. Collectively we are vibrating in an energy that is close to God, the *'I Am'* energy, the *'I AM Presence.''*

I asked Jesus, after everyone had left, "why do you feel it is so important to bring people together to discuss these topics - kindness, gratitude and love?"

"Well," replied Jesus, "do you not feel contented now, happy and joyful?"

"Yes, I do" I said, "I feel uplifted and motivated, I feel I could accomplish anything right now, there would be no stopping me, my vibration is high, yet I also feel such peace."

"Exactly!" Jesus said smiling. "This is why God wants people to come together, so that they feed off each other's high energy and joy, thus creating a circle which vibrates outward to the rest of society and the world. These good vibrations are catching, you know! People ask others, "why are you so joyful?" and reply, "I was with friends who talk of love and gratitude and I feel it, it carries with me when I leave their company." So they say, "oh, can I come with you next time and so it grows."

"So, is this like when we go the Temple?" I asked.

"No" replies Jesus, "the Temple at times can be inspiring and Holy, but on more occasions it cannot. It is just the rabbi preaching and condemning those who have missed a week or two. Or, condemning those who have not paid into the box. Or bringing children who may be crying or *'playing up'* during the service. Plus, the hierarchy of the places of worship is not as was wanted by my Father. The concept is indeed idealistic - that those who come to pray, do so for God - but to many, it may be a habit, just to be seen or out of fear of not going, which is no reason to attend at all."

"But, does it not say in the Commandments that there must be a day of rest to worship God?" I asked.

"Yes" replied Jesus, "it does, yet people take this so literally. A day of rest is a day spent as it says, resting, not working a paid job. It is time to give to the body space to relax. It is time to spend with family and friends. People may gather around a supper table, like we did tonight and discuss positive feelings and memories of the week past. They may thank God for the meal and the hands who made it, the farmers who brought it to the shops, the plants and animals who lived so that they can eat. This act is gathering in God's name, where all are equal and meet to rejoice in kindness, gratitude and love."

"So," I enquired, "you are saying, we don't have to go into a building of worship if we don't feel the need to?" "No, you don't. People connect with God/Source/Spirit in different ways. Many do so out in nature. They could be fishing, walking, or swimming in the sea or a lake. They may be in a garden, hugging a tree, sensing the birds, or walking their dog. Whatever people do that makes them feel connected, content and joyful, these activities are raising their vibration and are times when the vibration is even stronger." "In the place of worship then, what is happening here?" I said. "Oh, there are many Holy Men who talk of the truth of God," said Jesus, "but there are also many who feel superior as they preach to the people. Because they have studied the Bible, and as they put it, *'doing God's work'*, they feel that they have more knowledge about God than everyone else. Thus, they are superior and everyone else is inferior to them. They then make demands, make up rules and have the airs and graces that has everyone living in fear of being judged by them. This is not as God my Father wishes. No one is superior to anyone. Everyone is filled with the Divine Spark of God/Source/Spirit.

Everyone has that Light within them. No one - I repeat - no one, is any better because they have studied God's work. That is for fools, who have notions about themselves. Their egos have taken over and their power replaces their true essence which is love and Light.

I tell you now, little children are more connected to the Divine than these Holy Men who send the fear of God to the people. God is not, or never will, be something to fear. God energy is ONLY - I repeat - ONLY Love. Love and forgiveness, and that love of course, is unconditional love. Somewhere along the way these Holy Men have missed the whole point of God and worship. Somehow it becomes about laying down laws and controlling the masses. This is so far removed from what God wants for his people. The Universal energy of love is so pure that there is always more than enough for everybody. One day the world will finally realise this but that is a long, long way off, Peter. Many will come back many times before they realise this and learn the lessons of unconditional love."

Peter's Message
Love and Respect the God Within Yourself

What Jesus told me clearly when he was on earth, was that everybody is connected to God/Source/Spirit. No one has their lifetime here without the Creator making it happen. Therefore, everyone has the equal right to be this Divine energy. No one is better than anyone else in God's eyes.

Throughout the ages, before Jesus and after, this had not been so. There are religious institutions set up which, yes, have basically a true love of God and want to spread the word but they lose sight of what it's all about and why they formed their religion in the first place. Soon it becomes about building temples, churches, mosques, and teachings - with mainly men to serve God and the people - and then about manipulating rules and regulations, which are man-made, that the people must follow.

And if they don't follow these rules, they are told they are bad people - not worthy of being in the religion and not worthy of God's love.

I tell you now, this is nonsense. Jesus did not speak of rules and the 'do's and don'ts' about how and where, and how often to be with God. He spoke of love and forgiveness and joy, love of self and trusting one's own feelings, feelings of that one Divinity when one is connecting with the God within.

We watch now and are saddened by the hate, wars, famine and killings that have been caused in the name of religion. Why, we ask, can these fools not realise that they are not doing any of this in the name of God? They are doing it for selfish egotistical reasons, those which satisfy their own greedy need for power and control.

Some churches are now seeing this error in their ways. The Catholic Church for one has addressed and apologised for treating unmarried mothers so horrendously, implying it was a sin to have a child. This is just the opposite of what Jesus and God feel about a new life coming into the world. From a heavenly point of view too, any baby who passes over due to stillbirth, miscarriage or termination, comes straight to the Light. The controversy over termination is not for people on earth to judge, as God forgives all, and those who make decisions may regret it or not but will be joined with their baby again.

What we see now is a new energy coming into the world. There are many Light-workers, working to raise vibrations in a holistic way, a spiritual way that does not involve religious institutions with the many rules and regulations. Like those rules which determine who is fit to join and who is not. Families are breaking way from the religions they were brought up in, finding them restrictive and controlling. People are teaching their own children to love and respect the God within themselves, to be loving and kind and show this to ALL others. All this can be done, without attending any religious ceremony.

Parents are a spark of the Divine and they are capable of spreading the word of love, forgiveness, kindness and gratitude at home. Their own inner guidance, reading, discussions and inner wisdom is enough. Children may also learn about all religions at school, which gives them a broader prospective and lets them choose which way they want to go. Gone are the days of guilt and shame and talk of hell and damnation if you didn't obey God and go to church on Sunday.

God/Source/Spirit would rather see a family playing in a park or walking in the woods or on the beach, all enjoying each other, nature and giving thanks for the love and beauty that surrounds them. This is true love. This is appreciating all that is love, and in appreciating that, you are truly loving and connecting to God and the essence of the Universal love. You see, holding hands, in the park and giving thanks, means more to God than taking children to sit through a church service, where they are bored and restless and resent being there. Forcing children and people to attend religious institutions is not loving or kind. It actually turns those who grow up, and those who continue to attend services, to do so out of fear.

Going to church services out fear of what will happen to them if they don't go, is truly not in alignment with God. People attending religious services should only be there when they see it instead as a place of love.

So, what does Jesus say? He says what he has always said. Be with me always, be a rock. Be steadfast and solid in your faith, trusting that you are a spark of the Divine. Trust that you are part of God and that you will be guided by that all-knowing inner wisdom, especially when you are truly connected to the 'I AM Presence' within.

Jesus told me I was his rock, because of my faith, which had wavered at times but Jesus forgave me. He knew I was only human. Calling me the rock was a symbol of faith and trust by him in me. Everyone everywhere can be that rock when they are truly connected to God, reaching higher vibrations but staying grounded, steadfast and steady, on their journey here on earth.

It has been interpreted that when Jesus told me I was his rock upon which he would build his church, it meant one church, the only church.

I tell you now - Jesus meant we all have our own Church of God inside us. The physical building is only a symbol but one that has been misused by the power and hierarchy that surrounds it.

In the Catholic Church there have been Holy Popes, but there have also been very corrupt and controlling men in the Vatican City. We see a big shift in the present Pope Francis. He is a true man of God, who works from intuition, a place of Spirit, and is truly guided by God. As are we all - if we would only 'get out of our own way' and let it happen.

Letting go and letting God is when the rock within all of us is solid and our faith is unwavering, true and pure, which relates to all that really matters - pure unconditional love.

Forgiveness

Forgiveness: Jesus spoke so often to me and others about the importance of forgiving not only others but ourselves.

One day we were in the market. I was selling off my latest catch and there were many people about my stall. I had the money in a box underneath my table and as people paid I put the money in the box. At one point it was so busy, I left the box on the table and started working from there. From within the crowd a teenage boy ran over, grabbed the box and ran off with it. I didn't notice as I was busy packing up fish for a neighbour and we were having a friendly chat. Then I heard a man shout, "Peter, that boy has run off with your takings." I looked up and saw the back of his head, scampering off with my money box. I was furious. Jesus was nearby talking to some friends, so I called on him to watch my stall and I ran after this young man as fast as I could.

He was younger and fitter than me, so it wasn't easy to catch up with him, but I eventually did because he stumbled over some boxes. Then I want to grab him, another boy pushed me so I fell over and they both ran off.

I came back to my stall, so angry. Angry with these boys who had stolen my money and angry with myself because I had let them get away. My face flushed, I was talking loudly and banging my fists on the stall. "Why?" I shouted. "Why do this to me? I worked so hard to earn that money so that I can feed and clothe my family and for the upkeep of my boat. Who do these boys think they are? Do they know how to work for a living? Do they have to steal from others? This is sinful and not what God wants them to do. May they rot in hell for this."

Jesus was looking on. I could sense his presence, even though I was not facing him. I couldn't look him in the eye because I was angry, yet I was shameful of my reactions in front of him. Then I looked up, "what?" I said. "What am I to do? They stole from me. I am angry Jesus."

"I know you are Peter," Jesus replied. "And it is perfectly ok to be angry, that's a human emotion. You have to feel it, you have to let it out. If you don't let go of such emotions they become stuck inside you and eventually make you ill. So, let the anger out Peter. Go for a walk along the shore, where there are no people and roar and shout. Run up and down, if you wish, kick the sand, punch the air. Do what you need to do to release the anger. I'll stay here and look after your stall. Take your time, come back only when you feel the anger has released and you feel calm."

I did what Jesus said. I took myself off and walked where no one would hear me shout and scream. I kicked the sand and punched the air. I said words I would not utter in front of my children or my wife, or anyone for that matter.

I really, really felt the anger and resentment of these two teenage boys who had stolen my hard-earned money. Once I had let all my frustration out, I felt lighter. I started to breathe normally again instead of the fast-paced breaths of anger. Becoming aware of feeling lighter and my breaths slowing down, I felt a sense of relief and - although I couldn't quite fathom it - a sense of peace. But why would I feel peace? These boys robbed me, had taken from me what was rightly mine, not theirs. In having this thought, for a moment or two, I then started to feel some anger rise again. I felt it and then did a few more air punches, laughed at myself doing them and let it go.

In the laughter, I saw lightness and, in the lightness, I felt love. I felt love for my family and such gratitude that I had Sarah and the children and my fishing business to support them. I thought of the joy I feel every evening when I go home and they greet me and the love and warmth in our simple home. These feeling made me soften and I felt my original anger for the boys tone down a notch or two. "What must they be going through? I asked myself, "to have to go blatantly steal from me like that? They may have no food, a sick parent or sibling to feed. They may have no one to look after them and be a role model, thus they resort to stealing from others because they have no morals to measure for doing such a thing." It was in this reflection I saw the need for forgiveness but I was not at that place quite yet.

When I returned to my stall, Jesus was selling the rest of the catch and was smiling as he handed me the takings. "Well, there is still some to take home" he said, "so that's good news."

"I know," I replied, "but it still does not excuse what they did." He nodded in agreement and added, "you seem much calmer, did the walk and advice help? Did you punch the air, kick the sand, scream and shout?"

"Yes, I did and I feel so much better now that I got rid of all that anger. I've never done that before. It's a good tool. My own father used to take his anger out on us children. It wasn't pleasant. If only people knew that it's ok to be angry, but to just take it away and deal with it, and let it go, in a safe place, preferably alone."

"Were you able to see why these boys maybe did what they did, though that does not make it right." "Yes, I can," I said. "I got clarity when I released the anger and felt lighter. This led on to feelings of love and gratitude for my own family and friends. I feel for these boys who had to resort to doing this. But in future, I will take more care too and not leave the box on the table.

From now on I will wear a wallet tied around my waist or hang it around my neck."

"So," said Jesus, "can you forgive them?" I pondered for a moment or two. "Yes, I can," I said. "They need this money more than I do and I was obviously meant to leave the box on the table so that I could release the anger and forgive." Jesus smiled and nodded, "you have come far Peter. You have mellowed since we first met. I value your true Self coming out to play and stay. I value your friendship too."

A few days later I was at my stall in the market again, and a woman that I had never met before, came up to me. She had waited until the end of the day and I was just packing up. She was shabbily dressed and I thought she was looking for yesterday's fish - the ones I might throw back to the sea for the gulls. "Can I help you?" I asked her, "Can I help you?"

She replied, "I hope you will understand" and she handed me my box the boys had taken. I was taken aback. "How did you get that?" I asked. "My sons brought it to me as we have no money for food as my husband is very ill and we cannot work. We have ten children and the younger ones were crying out in hunger. So, the two older boys resorted to this," and she pointed to the takings box. I looked inside and it was empty.

"The money is gone," I said "that was my takings from my work, to feed my family." "I know," she replied, "and I am sorry. They used the money to buy supplies. Then when I finally got it out of the younger boy, where they got the money, I was very angry and said I would bring this back to you and offer their services to help you out and run your stall until it is paid back. They are ashamed and sorry for what they did." At that point the two boys came from behind a barrel, their heads down. "We apologise," said the older boy, "we were desperate, but our mother and father would not like us to live like this. Tell us how we can pay you back."

I was surprised. How many times in my life I had passed judgement and resentment and things never got resolved?

Now for the first time I had felt the feelings, then let go and forgiven these boys in my heart and look what happened. Not only did I get the box back (which had sentimental value as Sarah had carved it for me), but the boys apologised, saw the error of their actions and were willing to pay me back in service. I felt humbled. I accepted their offer and they helped me until the payment was completed. I got to know them and they stayed on to help me and I paid them, when need be. Looking at their circumstances had led me to have empathy, which lead to forgiveness and love. I thanked Jesus for his wisdom in the teachings of forgiveness.

Peter's Message
The Sweetness and Lightness of Forgiveness

In the Higher Realms we do not need to talk about, discuss or mention forgiveness because it is just a given that it is done, automatically. No need for forgiveness when there is only love. Love conquers all so there is no need for anything else.

On earth though it is a totally different matter. We see the hurts, the hate, the struggle for power and the need by so many to be right.

All these lead to feelings of anger, resentment, bitterness, revenge and hatred. With such dark feelings, how can anyone feel anything but the opposite of love? Forgiveness does not even come into their radar.

In his teaching, Jesus talks about forgiveness and how crucial it is to come home to oneself. Many people's biggest problem is about forgiving themselves for past acts and misdemeanours, thus keeping them disconnected from Source.

My own feelings on forgiveness, before I met Jesus, were very different from what I came to believe. I was taught by my father, and he by this father before him, that forgiveness was to be weak and was seen by others as a weakness. It was viewed as a womanly thing, not for men, especially when they were head of the household.

In my former years before Jesus, I would get angry and bear grudges. I would keep the anger. That's because I learned from my father, and he from his, and so on. It was such a relief to find the sweetness and lightness of forgiveness. We may not condone the sins, but once we let go of them with forgiveness, then we can move on. Only the letting go, the act of forgiveness will set us free. It's what Jesus came on earth to do, and now with his second coming through Christ Consciousness in this higher vibrational time, it is what makes forgiveness happen.

Light workers are spreading the word through their ability to touch the lives of others. They understand, like the mysteries, how the old ways of resentment, judgement and jury are not the ways of God/ Source/Spirit. In coming now at this time, they can bring Light in a forever-changing world, which at times seems so full of darkness. These times of darkness are opportunities for communities to come together and for people worldwide to unite in the quest of love and forgiveness - because the forgiveness brings the love, which in turn leads to the Light.

I tell you now, only those who have forgiveness in their hearts can truly be at one with God, for it is the very part of them that is that, which is unconditional love.

Adolescents

Not only did Jesus love to be in the company of children, but he loved to be with young people too. The adolescent years, as he called them, were both confusing and exciting times and he enjoyed conversing with teenagers in the village.

Now most teenagers would find adult company dull and prefer to be in their own circle of friends, but not surprisingly, it was very different when Jesus was around. Young people would gather around him. You would hear them shouting to their friends, "come quickly, Jesus is in the market", or "Jesus has just come out of his workshop", or "here comes Jesus and Peter." It would make me smile and I would feel Jesus' energy as he would be in such joy at having them call out for him. Both boys and girls came to talk with him and he treated them both equally, not making the boys feel superior or more important like many other men did in the village at the time.

One particular day one of the boys asked Jesus, "what do adults think about us?" and "why do they want to tell us what do and how we should shape our future?"

"What wonderful questions!" he replied. "Firstly, all adults have been teenagers, some remember it's a challenging time, others tend to block these years out and pretend they were always adults, who do not want to look deeper at their own lives and yet have pleasure in ridiculing other people. Those who do not recall these years will have no empathy. And although being a parent will trigger unresolved issues of their own youth, this gives them ample opportunity - under self-reflection - to readdress them, feel the pain, then release and heal. And through this healing, they will progress further on their spiritual journey."

"So, what do adults think of you? Some will understand what you are going through, many will choose to forget what it is like to do so, like their parents before them and so the patterns continue."

"And why do adults want to tell you what to do and how to shape your future? Well, that dear soul, is twofold. Firstly, they think they know what is best for you. They want you to do well, be happy and secure. That's why parents find it so difficult to let their children grow up. They want to keep you safe and protect you. That is their instinct and their duty. Yet they tend to forget that you don't belong to them as such. You are children of the Universe, from Source/Spirit/God. You are on loan to them on earth, to be cared for until you can leave home and fend for yourselves."

"This time of adolescence is different for both the young people and adults' relationships. It is a great test for parents to wake up and show how their own journey is now not being reflected back to them when they have their own parental reactions."

"The main reason for parents wanting to tell you what to do is love. It's just not always the unconditional love that my Father gives everybody. Many parents have so many conditions tied into their roles with their children, especially for those aged 13 plus."

The crowd of adolescents sitting around Jesus had grown since the young boy had asked the questions. Word was spreading fast in the village that he was talking about and interested in them. He was a breath of fresh air, compared to all the other adults they knew, where they felt tolerated and loved of course, but never really listened to.

Then a young girl of about of about 14 or 15, said, "Jesus, what does God expect of us?" Jesus smiled, "my dear child, for that is what we all are, Children of God. He expects you to be nothing more or nothing less than you. You - magnificent you. When you remember connecting to God, then that is everything, nothing else is important. Once you have that truth, belief, connection and trust, God/Source/Spirit will guide you through life, but you must be willing to look, listen and feel for this guidance."

"So how do I do that Jesus?" "Well, you must tune into being in the vibration where you can hear God's voice, and this is done in silence." "Silence?" "Yes" Jesus replied. "Silence. When you sit in silence, you are closest to God, you can hear his voice calling you to guide you on your journey. You will hear words, these will be backed up by signs, as you live daily and notice what seems as coincidences but are synchronicities, confirming you are on the right path. But mostly you will feel, really feel what is right for you and what is not, what brings you joy and fills your heart with love and what does not. Follow the feeling as they are what your soul is telling you, and your soul is the real you, the part of you that never dies and is always connected to the I AM Presence, God."

"So, are you saying that God wants me to follow his words and not those of my parents? I want to learn to build but my parents say that is for a boy to learn to do. My brothers are out working with my father and I am meant to stay with my mother and sew. I don't like to sew, it bores me, but I love to build things, construct and see the final outcome. It excites me, makes me happy, fulfils me, gives me joy."

"Well" replied Jesus, "that is your passion and you have to follow it." "But that means going against my parent's wishes." "Well, that is what you must do then. If you feel something so strongly and it is God's wish for you as part of your soul's plan, then you must pursue it. Respect your parents' concerns but convince them of your passion and joy, for that is what makes you whole, and in this wholeness, you are connected to God."

Jesus continued talking and listening to the young people for many hours. Someone brought him some food and water, even a mother arrived with a blanket when it became dusk.

"You are such a positive influence and a teacher and role model to our young people," she said. "They may be reaching adulthood, but they are still children to us mothers, it is hard to let them go. It's because we love and care for them that we hang on and try to guide them with the rules and regulations."

Jesus smiled and said, "yes, by all means have boundaries but always remember, your children are not yours to keep, they are Children of the Universe, as are you and only on loan until they can fend for themselves.

Peter's Message
Positive Parenting with Unconditional Love

It has always been clear that these adolescent years are the most difficult as the physical body is changing. Mentally and emotionally the child is too.

We see a big change in today's world as many young people are stepping into their power and leading with conviction about what and where they need to go. This is good, especially where they follow their hearts.

We see so many lost young people. Lost souls – all looking for connections and competing with the media and the social media view of them - in this world filled with egos and unacceptable expectations.

This is where the parents come in as role models. This is also where it is difficult, as their own role models (the grandparents) have been disconnected for so long, that they offer no assistance or guidance.

Jesus always talked to the teenagers' parents about their roles in the positive parenting or Godlike parenting as it was called then. Jesus would say, "my Father would not scream or shout at me or any of you. He would talk calmly and always remind us how much He loved us, no matter what we do. This must be related to young people as they are going through so much - physically, mentally and emotionally. They must always be certain that they need to hear it and feel it every single day. This is every parent's most important and valuable job in their lifetime.

Today we see young people strive to both fit in and express themselves but it is so much harder than ever before with the worldwide web making everything so instant and accessible. There is much instant gratification, while patience seems to be a thing of the past for these young people. It is up to the adults to guide them, yet how do they do that when this younger generation craves instant gratification, and constant comparison and showing off too. We do not know what to make of it all in the Higher Realms, but we do know that it can't continue. Such demands and competiveness destroy souls and this does not lead people to be connected to God! Jesus came here to connect.

Jesus came to teach about love. Love comes in many forms and for most parents, it can be challenging to remember this unconditional love in times of teenage anger, stubbornness, rudeness and what is deemed as lack of respect. But I tell you now, the parents must be the adults here, and be with their teenagers from an unconditionally loving perspective, with the knowledge and understanding that this phase will pass. And have the wisdom to have the patience and kindness and meet their demanding behaviour with all the love in their hearts. This is what we ask, this is what Jesus would do and this is what God/Spirit/Source asks of parents and adults all over the world. Do not take advantage of these young people: respect where they are. You too were in this place. Always remember that.

CHAPTER

12

Divine Essence

Divine Essence is within all of us. Jesus' teachings tell this but many take these teachings in the Bible and use them literally to condemn those who may perceive them in their own way.

On a summer's evening Jesus was in the garden with myself, Sarah and our children. Joshua was playing with clay and stones and Maria was smelling the flowers she had picked to give to Mother Mary. She was arranging them in a little posy, and it looked so pretty. She handed them to Jesus saying, "please give them to your lovely Mama." Jesus hugged our little girl and sat her on his knee. It was then I noticed Joshua was looking very sad. "What's wrong son," I asked. "Nothing!" and he scowled.

"We know that it is something Joshua, you have both a cross and a sad face," said Sarah. Then he got up from where he was sitting and ran to the bottom of the garden, he folded his arms and I could tell he was about to cry.

"Let me talk to him," said Jesus. He placed Maria on my knee and walked down towards Joshua.

Twenty minutes later, they both walked back up towards us hand in hand, laughing as they walked and talked. Then Joshua ran over to his clay and stones again and the pots he was putting them into.

"So, whatever that was about Jesus, you certainly fixed it," I said. He smiled and said nothing. We continued to chat and Sarah was telling us of her latest creation with wood, when Joshua stood in front of us, handed a pot to Jesus and said, "please give this to your lovely mother. Tell her it's from me, Joshua, and that I made it especially for her, with much love."

"Well, thank you Joshua," replied Jesus, my mother will be delighted with your wonderful gift and Maria's sweet smelling and beautiful flowers."

Joshua smiled and said to Sarah and I. "Mama and Papa, do you see the gorgeous pot of stones I have made, it is beautiful, and just as beautiful - but in a different way - to the flowers Maria has picked and arranged.

"Oh, indeed they are," said Sarah tenderly.

Joshua added, "I was upset earlier because I thought my gift for Mother Mary was not as good as Maria's. I thought hers was better than mine. However, Jesus explained to me that everyone is different and they express love and beauty in very different ways and that is good. He said *'wouldn't it be boring if everyone and everything and every idea were all the same.'* Just because my stones in the pot may be duller in colour and not have the pleasant smell of the flowers, they are interesting to look at and they have so many textures when you take them out and hold them in your hand. That's still beauty, and my gift was made by me. I used my imagination, it's unique and I made it with love." He was so pleased with his speech; he was grinning from ear to ear.

"Jesus said that it's not what you have made or how it even looks, it's the loving thoughts that go into it while making it that makes the difference. That's what God tells Jesus too, and he should know because he is God." We laughed at his closing remark. Then I thanked Jesus for settling our son, who could be quite critical with himself at times. We had sensed he got nervous around making things perfect so that he could get recognition.

Jesus made it clear to him that if you do what you do from a place of love, everything is beautiful.

After the children were in bed we continued our chat about the importance of coming from our centre - that place of love, our Divine aspect, the Light within - which means we are coming from a place of God in all our thoughts and actions. In doing so Jesus said, "we can only be love in the eyes of God and thus in that of others."

It was Sarah who challenged him. "But Jesus, how can that be so, when so many people do criticise when we do not do things the way they do. Take for example, me working in the workshop with you two to three days a week. I do this because I love to work with wood and be creative, it makes me so happy, it fulfils me, it's is my passion. Yet there are many men and women in the village who do not approve, as they view my role only as a mother. In their eyes, that is where I should be all time, home with my children and cooking and cleaning and doing nothing else but caring for my husband and family. There are men and women who have stopped speaking to me. You know that I am only doing what I am doing because of love, both following my passion and love for my family.

Jesus replied, "you are doing what your heart desires Sarah, that is following your bliss and that is what love is all about. You came here to be human, to fall in love with Peter, have children and follow your dreams to be creative with wood. That is your plan and to go against it, no matter what people say or don't say to you, is to go against God/Source/Spirit. You feel the love for how you live and in what you do – that confirms that you are following your soul's path by fulfilling your heart's desire.

We watched Jesus' love daily - love for all people, places, plants and animals. Love in his actions too, as all his actions came from a place of love. Jesus saw many things coming from a place of love, and many things that did not, but he always saw ways of turning them around and voicing his views on how everything could be changed if coming from love.

One day a man asked him for coins. Jesus put his hand in his pocket and gave some money to the man - all he had actually. The man didn't even thank him, he just grabbed the money and ran. "Why did you not chastise him?" I said. "He was so ungrateful." I did not give the money for thanks," Jesus replied. "I gave it out of love, for a fellow who needed it more than I." "But did he?" I asked. "We'll never know," replied Jesus "yet, we know that he is loved."

Jesus and I had many wonderful conversations before he started his ministry and recruited me and the 11 Apostles to assist him. On many occasions he would say, "Simon Peter, my words and actions will be scripted and man will interpret them in many ways.

"What do you mean?" I asked. "Well, in years to come, people - mainly men - will use my teachings to control the masses. They will take my teachings that have been scripted (and not always correctly) to make up their own rules so that they have power, not the people.

People do not realise they have their own Divine Essence within, though they seek this understanding and guidance from those who themselves are indoctrinated by religious restrictions, sharing their fear, and manipulating through lies and corruption. They will tell people that they are sinful, not good enough, that they will go to hell. It breaks my heart that this will happen and continue for thousands of years after I leave this earth. And those who teach that God is only of fire and brimstone and damnation are so, so wrong. They will create fear and much sadness, anxiety and unhappiness for so many people."

"So how can we ensure this won't happen?" I asked.

"We can't," he replied. "It is how it is meant to be. The world will have to be. The world will have to be like this, until the second coming - when I will not come back physically but

Heaven will send Light-workers who will assist in the opening of hearts, minds and souls to the power of unconditional love. And the love will be spread through many ways, and so far removed from the traditional ways that are deemed the normal way to worship God. It will be less about worship and more about connecting with the Divine Essence within, which is what I will have taught at the very beginning, but others chose to change it and make up their own rules to give themselves the power to lead the people in fear. The Christ Consciousness that will become so apparent and so, so strong 2,000 years after I depart will be what saves humanity from distractions. and so it is."

Peter's Message
Changing to Unconditional Love Will Change Humanity

In coming to say these truths now, through an ordinary woman to scribe, I can honestly say that Jesus believes everyone is equal. From the Higher Realms we observe and feel the energy of all that is unconditional love, a love so powerful that humans cannot truly sense it, and it will not be felt until the transition home. On knowing it is the only truth - the truth of God/Source/Spirit vibrating through this Christ Consciousness - we pray that this time of enlightenment can benefit humanity and reach all those who are willing to feel it and are awakened to this higher energy which promotes only love.

> *Love, not hate.*
> *Love, not bigotry.*
> *Love, not war.*
> *Love, not competitiveness.*
> *Love, not superiority.*
> *Love, not fear.*
> *Love, not extreme wealth and severe poverty.*
> *Love, not ego.*
> *Love, not selfishness.*
> *Love, not self-absorption.*
> *Love, love, love!*

This message of love, this truth, this only truth may seem lost in today's world, a world that still hears, feels and sees unnecessary wars and much suffering. This suffering is so uncalled for and yet against it is man's need for power and greed that causes these wars. This is why we need the Divine Feminine to rise. It is rising but more and more will tap into this energy - men too - and this will make such a difference to the world as it is now. We see and feel the pain that these wars bring, but be assured, those who are involved and are victims to these dire circumstances have chosen this path in this incarnation. Whatever lessons they have wanted to learn, or human suffering they endure, will be acted out in this lifetime and redeemed and reclaimed in the next.

War brings much sadness, pain and suffering and these vibrations are felt around the world. Those involved have disconnected from their Light within, which is God/Spirit/Source. This disconnection from their true being will bring only hurt and despair, a huge lesson to learn when the time comes for transition to the Light.

In today's world, we see so much happening in the news and in social media, and while some information is good, too much information that is dark causes the vibration to lower, especially when we get caught up in passing remarks and commenting constantly about things that are not of concern. Yes, by all means speak out about what you believe in, but always do this from a place of love. Being love-centred and heart-centred and coming from a place of empathy and understanding are the only ways to be in this world, which at times seems so very dark. Yet we can assure you that change is happening. More and more people are turning to the Light within, to Source/Spirit/God and remembering to love like Jesus did, in love - pure unconditional love.

13

Authenticity

Jesus always gave of himself to others - his True Self - not how he thought others would like him to be. An example of this was one day when we were fishing and my brother Andrew asked Jesus to help bring in the nets.

Jesus was tired. He had been working late in his workshop and had been up early to help us as we had a big catch coming in. As Andrew threw the rope to draw in the net, Jesus reached over, slipped and fell into the water. We panicked, we weren't even sure if he could swim and he seemed to be nowhere to be seen, as he had gone under. I shouted his name but there was no response. "Andrew," I called, "look at the other end, quick, where is he? Jesus! Jesus!" I cried.

Still there was no sound, only the lapping of the water against the boat. We were the only boat out, so I could not even shout for help. It was very distressing indeed.

Then, what seemed like hours, but was probably only minutes, Jesus appeared at the other end of the boat. But he just stepped out of the water as if it was a step.

"The nets are full," he said. "And there are enough fish for you to have the rest of the week off to spend with your families," he added.

I smiled, as I knew this was Jesus and he could do what was extraordinary.

Andrew stood and then sat down in disbelief. "What just happened?" he said. "One minute you are reaching for the rope, next you slip, fall in, minutes later step out on top of the water and tell us the nets are overflowing and to take the rest of the week off. This is not normal. It is the talk and actions of a crazy man."

He put his hands on his head and kept shaking his head, repeating, "what is going on, am I seeing things?"

"No" replied Jesus. "You are not. I am the Son of God; therefore, I can perform what others cannot do as I am in the same vibration as my Father. You too can do many things, yet, you do not think you have the power within you as you are so caught up in the densities of the world. For the moment, I am not telling people who I am, only certain people know. Those who love and support me know who I am. When the time comes, we will spread the world about God's Light and Love. Would you care to join us?"

Andrew looked over at me, "why brother, did you not tell me about your friend Jesus? You have known for a while now, I'm sure, that he is the Son of God."

"Andrew," I replied, "it was not my story to tell. Jesus has been living among us on earth in human form. He wants to experience it fully before he starts his mission."

"Andrew," Jesus said, "you have not answered my question. Will you not answer my question? Would you like to join myself and Peter and other good men and women, when we go to spread the word of God?"

Andrew, who was still a little stunned, replied, "of course I would Jesus, it would be an honour. I thank you for being truly you today and showing me you as the Son of God. I will go where you ask of me and whatever you wish me to do, I will do - to tell others about your life on earth and how you are here to teach the word of God."

"Thank you, Andrew. When the time is right, you will be with us. I will tell you now that our teaching will be of how God is a God of Love, unconditional love, not a God of fear that has been deemed falsely by many. Love will rejoice as we seek to spread the good news of the heavenly Father of joy, kindness, compassion, forgiveness and love.

Another occasion when Jesus took a loved one by surprise was when we had a birthday party for Joshua. It was his 7th birthday and he had some friends over to play. We made his favourite food and the children played as Sarah and I, Jesus and Mary and his mother Mary and some friends sat talking and then attending to the children when need be. They wanted to play alone, without the adults as they told us they had more fun. Joshua made a special request though," after we play for a while, will you come and join us, Jesus?"

"Of course, I will," Jesus replied, "Call me when you are ready."

In the meantime, Maria, who was four, decided she wanted to play with the boys too. She had a little friend with her, one of the boy's sisters, and they were having fun but decided that joining the big boys would be better. She made her way over, her little friend in tow and they giggled, happy to be able to play with their brothers. But, as one can imagine, Joshua was not pleased. "Go away Maria," he shouted, "you and Esme are not allowed to play with us, it's a boy game." I was about to intervene and ask her to come away when Jesus said, "do you mind Peter, if I step in?" "Not at all," I replied. "Be my guest. This is a tough call," and I smiled.

So, Jesus took over, in the gentle and calming way that is him in his essence. "Joshua, may I now join you and your friends? Jesus asked. "Oh yes, please!" exclaimed Joshua and his little friends cheered. "Let the man play, but not those silly girls!" said one of the boys called Daniel.

"So why do you say that Daniel? Jesus asked. "Well, girls are no good at games." Daniel replied. "And they aren't as smart or as strong as us boys." At this point Joshua's face fell, as he knew this was not something we ever said in our house.

Jesus said nothing. He just beckoned the 2 little girls to come over and he put his arms around each of them. "Let's play boys!" he said, "two teams, the girls and the boys and I'm in the girls' team. Let's see who is smart and strong but I bet you the girls are up there, so you better get ready."

Jesus called Sarah to be in their team too and I was the judge. The other adults cheered everyone on as they played races, throwing, jumping, hiding and creating. It was a full-on couple of hours and by the end of it all, everyone was exhausted.

"So!" said Joshua, "who won? Who is smarter and stronger? Us boys." The boys cheered, thinking they had won a prize.

"Peter, how did both teams do?" Jesus asked. I weighed up all the activities and realised that both teams had excelled in different areas. Yes, the boys had been faster in their race but the girls were more creative in their stone pattern game.

"It's a draw!" I said. The little boy Daniel was very cross. "That's not fair," he said. "My father says boys are much smarter and stronger, we are meant to win, not stupid girls."

"We are not stupid," Maria cried out. Esme was quiet, "but boys are better" she said.

"Now stop all that now!" said Jesus, and it's the first time I'd heard him raise his voice, though he did so kindly. "Do you know that God sees boys and girls as equals, you are both the same in His eyes because he is also she.

We call God, God our Father in Heaven, but God is also our Mother in Heaven. God is both him and her. So why would God ever think boys are better than girls, when He/She is both - they are equal."

The adults who did not realise who Jesus was, looked on, surprised and disbelieving.

"How do you know this?" said Daniel. You are making this up, that's called telling lies, that is bad."

"I tell you now. I have not made this up Daniel, because I am the Son of God and God tells me. I know this and He asks me to tell you. Soon I will be travelling to tell people about

God's Word, I will take followers who believe with me and they too will spread the word of God."

"Can I come with you Jesus?" said Joshua. "I know you are the Son of God, I feel it from you, your energy is all about love. You are so kind and I know that Maria is the same as me, I am no better because I am a boy." I know God is good and He /She loves us all.

Jesus smiled "You can come someday, when we go locally Joshua, as you will have to stay and help your mother and Maria when your father is away with me. I would also like you to spread the word to the other children. Tell them that it is good to be kind to one another, boys and girls, and that God loves everyone the same.

The little boy Daniel was not taking this in. He looked very puzzled and walked right up to Jesus and said, "so, Jesus, if this is your mother and he pointed to Mother Mary, how can God be your Father and Mother?"

Jesus smiled and said, "young man, you are very inquisitive and your logical mind cannot take in this information, which is what happens here on earth. But I tell you now, Mother Mary is my earth mother. She gave birth to me so I could experience this on earth. My earthly father Joseph, a very kind and loving man, has now gone to join my heavenly Father. My heavenly Father is both Father and Mother to everyone, the energy from God is a balanced male and female energy/vibration. It is just the way it is. God gives us logic and imagination. Logic is useful and imagination is everything. Believing what cannot be seen, but what is felt and imagined, is what keeps the world going and will do for the thousands of years to come."

At that point Jesus whistled and a dozen wild birds came to rest on him. He held out his arms while they lined up, one was on his head.

"Would you like one on your head?" he said to all of the children. "Oh yes!" they all replied.

He whistled again and six of the birds flew to rest on the children's heads and they rested on their arms and allowed the children to pet them. The other six birds stayed with Jesus.

"So, Daniel, do you believe that I am the Son of God, that God in Heaven is both Father and Mother and that He/She loves everyone equally?"

"Oh yes Jesus! I do, I do, I do! Let me help Joshua spread the word about you and God. God is good and loves us all. I know now I want to be like him and you."

Peter's Message
Take Time to Be Your Authentic Loving Self

It is very clear in this chapter that Jesus was, and is always, true to himself and this is what he wishes for everyone. Nowadays there are so many pressures in the world with image and material things. Having to constantly let the world know where you are, who you are with and what you are up to that people don't feel they can be their true authentic selves. This is because they don't find time to be, to be alone, reflect, feel their feelings, notice the triggers and have acceptance about who they really are.

Until Jesus took himself and the Apostles on his ministry, he was living among us, not preaching and teaching as such, but living fully in the present moment in love. Those who did not know yet that he was the Son of God knew, however, that there was something very special about him and that he was different in many ways. Just being in his presence made people feel loved. It's hard to describe this now, but his energy really was of such a higher vibration. It was sacred and people just felt it.

Once Jesus started his ministry, this all made sense to those who had met him and would hear people say, "I always felt he was no ordinary man."

Jesus was adamant in his teachings that no one was ordinary when they tapped into their own Divine Light within and understood that they too were a spark of God. By doing this and believing in the mystery of that which cannot be seen, true glory and joy are what we feel. Trust that this Higher Power/Divine Intelligence/Source/Spirit/God will guide you throughout life, if you only take time to listen and to feel and look for the signs that lead you on your path.

Many times, Jesus talks of this. There are many quotes in the Bible. However, there seems to be vast differences between many different religions on how Jesus taught of God and love.

I tell you now, I have said it before here in this scribing and I say it again. God loves everyone, unconditionally, whether we believe or not. There are many who only believe out of fear, because their religions say they should. Many believe in nothing, saying there is no God. Why would the world be the way it is (wars, famine, violence), if that was the case? Many believe in only science, they can't explain or see God, so they say he is made up and that the stories about Jesus are fabricated to keep people in check.

I tell you now - God exists. Jesus walked on earth and the Apostles and I were with him and witnessed it all. Man's interpretations of the Bible leave a lot to be desired in many cases. Those who see God as a loving God - a God of pure unconditional love - are correct. Those who fear him and judge others are not.

Jesus taught about love and forgiveness and tolerance for everyone. What people do on earth is the basis of their love for themselves and in that, their love for God, that Divine Spark within.

Life Lessons

I recall a time when we were walking home from a fishing trip. Again, Jesus had come to help me, as he said he loved the peace and serenity out on the water and we, of course, enjoyed each other's company. Sometimes we would chat, other times we would sit in silence, only communicating when it was time to bring the nets in and we needed to talk. It got to a stage when we didn't even have to do talk, because we knew each other so well. It was as if we could read each other's minds and the communication was therefore intuitive and non-verbal.

Anyway, on our way home Jesus spoke to an older man on the side of the road. He was wearing ragged clothes and sitting on a rock with a cloth bag at his feet. His feet were dirty, as he had no shoes. He was eating a piece of fruit and he smiled as Jesus addressed him.

"How are you this fine day?" Jesus asked.

"I am very good," replied the man. "I have food to eat, the sun is shining and you have stopped to say hello. How kind of you, I thank you for doing so," he replied. I smiled at him too, and nodded acknowledgement.

"Do you mind if I ask you something?" Jesus asked. "Not at all," said the man.

Jesus asked, "you look so happy, yet you have ragged clothes, no shoes and a bag at your feet. May I ask what makes you smile?" "Life," he replied. "I am indeed very blessed. Many would not see this as such as I have much misfortune in my life. Some years ago, I lost my wife and little baby daughter. My wife died during childbirth. Then my only remaining child - my older son, who was four at the time - became ill and I lost him 4 months later. I was, of course, devastated. It was bad enough to lose my wife and daughter but to lose my son too - the one thing that was keeping me sane, was incomprehensible and so cruel. I was angry, angry with God, angry with life. But this anger just made me a horrible person. I was a successful businessman before I lost my family. In my grief and anger I caused ripples which destroyed other people's lives too. I could not bear to see other people happy, so I made their lives miserable by letting go of employees and overcharging customers. I was not a nice man - I was horrible, in fact.

Then one day, a year after my son had passed, and sixteen months after I lost my wife and daughter, a man came into my market, with his wife alongside a five-year-old boy and a little girl, who was just over a year old. The boy was laughing and holding his father's hand. The wife was carrying the girl who was lovingly stroking her mother's face. Then the little girl reached out her arms to come to me and the boy ran over and said, "my sister never goes to anyone but my mother and father, so you must be very special." As he said that, he wrapped his arms around my leg and gave me a hug. This was the moment that changed everything. As I held this little girl in my arms and the boy hugging my legs, I realised this was my boy and girl telling me - through these children who were the same age - that they were ok, that they loved me and that although they were not with me physically, this sign of affection was them, showing me I was loved.

I knew at that point I had to change my ways. I asked the family could I take them to lunch. They came to my home, my housekeeper made us a feast and I told this man and his wife my story. They were a lovely couple. They were new to the area and he was looking for work here and was working in the markets. It turned out that he was a bright man with good business sense and a kind heart. I knew God had sent this family to me. I knew what I had to do. I asked him to look after my business for a year, to live in my home with his family, and I would return to them when I was ready but that I wanted them to stay and make this their home.

The next day I took a bag of clothes and left with what I was wearing and began to travel. I am travelling to make amends. I will visit those whom I have hurt in my year of anger and grief. I will work for nothing for them, with food as pay. I will serve others as I am sorry for how I treated people. My wife and children gave me such joy. Although I only held my daughter for an hour before she passed, that hour was one I will never forget. The pain of losing them all will never leave but I have to accept it and be thankful for the time I had with them all.

I choose now to smile, to be thankful and rejoice in the family who showed me to be this way instead of continuing the rest of my life in suffering. I will wander and help others with no money or rewards. Only when I feel I have learned what life is to be happy, with nothing, with nobody, and only being of service, will I know what it is like to be true to myself and God. These lessons I must have chosen before I came to earth. I will live in peace again."

"Thank you telling us your story," said Jesus. I looked on in a complete state of sympathy. I could not, for a moment, comprehend losing Sarah, Joshua and Maria. Yet here was this man now living his life and making amends to those he had hurt during his year of grief.

"But surely people will understand why you acted this way, why you hurt them? - you were angry and so terribly sad," I said.

"Yes, I have thought of that but people do not deserve to be treated badly because of my misfortune. It was not their fault that I lost my wife and new-born daughter, and then four months later my son. They did not cause this to happen, so why would I be so unkind and hurtful to them? I am so sorry now for what I did. I will spend as long as it takes for them all to forgive me and then I can forgive myself. In giving everything up to the family that mirrors mine, I have already begun to heal. In giving and loving, I am feeling the love of my family who are just gone from the physical world, yet here with me always. When my time comes to pass, we will meet again."

Jesus stood beside this man - who told us he was called Issac - and laid one hand on his shoulder and one on his heart. "Issac, I am the Son of God," he said. Issac smiled and replied, "I know, I can feel it, I knew you were someone from the Heavenly Realms and I sensed the Son of God. I feel honoured to be in your presence."

"I tell you Issac, this encounter between us had been planned, just as losing your family was too. It was their choice to come and go as they did. You signed up for this too, before you came to earth. Your wife and children are with you on your path. They are helping you heal. And they are at peace. They have gone home to God. They are with my Father. Understand this Issac, there is no more a beautiful place to be; in this physical world we can have glimpses of it, but only glimpses of the unconditional love and bliss of this. Being still, being love, being kind, compassionate, being forgiving are all earthly emotions and actions we can take to feel here on earth what will be so in Heaven."

"The pain of losing them is still there, but the pain of how I have treated others is almost worse" said Issac. "This is why I had to leave my home, business and go on my travels, wearing only rags and a bag on my back. It feels good to have nothing, live simply, and trust God will guide me as I make amends."

"How long have you been doing this now?" I asked.

"For two years," Issac replied.

"Well Issac," Jesus said, "it is time to go home. You have done your time. You have done your time of mourning and making amends. My Father forgives you but you know that because you have now forgiven yourself, haven't you?"

"I have," he replied. "That is why when I met you today I was able to say life is good. It is the first time I have said it in over three years. I am at peace with losing my family and for my actions."

"You are a wise man, Issac," said Jesus. "You have learned your lessons and you are ready to move on. I tell you, you will meet a woman to love again and while you will not forget your first wife and family, you will now go on to marry again and have a family to love, and from now on, you will always treat everyone you meet with such kindness and love."

Issac's eyes filled up with tears. "Thank you, thank you," he said. I will tell many of our meeting about love and listening to God."

Peter's Message
Life Mirrors Back to You How You Are Inside

It is always clear in Jesus' teachings that love is above all the only way to be in the world. Those who live by love will see this mirrored to them in so many ways. Those who don't live by love will, at many stages in their lives, be given the chance to, and mend the errors of their ways. Like the man we met who had turned his grief into anger and resentment, he was confronted by love from the children, and therefore it highlighted what he needed to do to change.

Many may not change. They will continue to live lives of a destructive nature - lives filled with anger, greed, terror and ugliness. These acts, of course, will be mirrored back to them and so the cycle continues. If only these people could see what we see and know. They too are filled with love and Light. They too come from Source energy. They too are capable of so much love - unconditional love, which they can give to others and receive in return. Only when humankind can see this true essence, will the world stop the wars, famine, greed and destructive patterns which are destroying the planet.

In this time of Higher Consciousness, however, many are waking up. It is a time of awakening and through this awakening, those who choose to be on this path will be living in a higher vibration and they in turn will affect the world in many ways.

Jesus came and left so that the world would grow and develop, not only in material ways but also in consciousness. This is that time when the Christ Consciousness is at its highest, and many unsettling things are happening in the world all the time to make room for this higher vibration, and the Light of those who are bringing in the higher energies.

This may seem very 'fluffy' but I assure you now, we have all been prepared for this time of great change. The unsettling times ahead will bring only great joy to the world once the 'shake up' has settled, and God's children realise that unconditional love is the only way.

CHAPTER 15

The Divine Spark

When Jesus and I would have our deep and meaningful talks about life and the work he came on earth to do, he would always remember, "I am not my thoughts."

I would, at the start when he'd say this, be very confused. "But what do you mean Jesus?" I asked. "How can that be? I am constantly thinking, especially when I am alone and my mind wades to both past events and the future."

"Yes, I know," he said, "but what you don't realise is that you can stop that and keep your thoughts in the present, in the now, as this is the only time you have."

"But that's impossible," I replied. "I'll be thinking about something that happened that morning, when I am out fishing, about how another fisherman was rude to me, or Sarah and I had cross words over breakfast or how my father said something to me that pressed my buttons. I find myself living in the past a lot. Plus, I do worry about the future, about how the children will do at school, will we have enough to support them, will there always be enough fish, what if my boats need fixed and I can't afford it, what if Sarah took ill and I had to rear the children on my own. These are the many thoughts that would go through my head daily. How do I stop these Jesus? Is this not normal?"

"Yes, it is normal for men, women and older children to do this. You will observe younger children though, they don't do this to the same extent. Actually, babies don't do this at all. They live in the now - everything, every thought is present moment. We were all babies once. Even now at four, Maria will not worry about things, her life is very present moment. Let me show you."

We were at my home, so we called Maria who was playing outside.

"Maria, what are you doing now?" Jesus asked. She jumped on his knee and gave him a hug "I am smiling at you and giving you a hug," she said. I smiled.

"Before that, what were you doing?" Jesus said.

"Well, I was playing outside, building a house of sticks and stones."

"What were you thinking when you were doing this?" he asked.

"About the sticks and stones and where they would go."

"Did you think of anything else while doing this?"

"I did think, this will be so lovely when it is finished and I can't wait to show Joshua and his friends. That's all."

"Are you hungry?"

"No." Maria replied. "If I was hungry I would come in and say *'Is dinner ready?'* I wouldn't just think about it, I'd ask."

We laughed and she said, "is that all. Can I go outside again now?"

"Of course," Jesus replied. "You are such a beautiful child, full of Light, full of love."

"Thank you," she said. "I love you father and Jesus," and off she went.

"So, Peter, can you see and hear what I mean? Maria, when she does anything, it is in the now as she does it. When she is playing outside, she is not thinking about what happened yesterday or what she'll do tomorrow, she just plays. She will continue in this way of being for another few years and then she will start to think about the past and the future, especially from adolescence onwards.

At this stage, being in the now just keeps her so connected to God/Source/Spirit. Being present is what being Godly is all about. It's about connecting in with that vibration that keeps us close to the Creator/All That Is/I AM Presence. Children are the closest on earth to the Heavenly Father

I understand this Jesus," I replied, "but how do I keep my mind from wandering, worry and trying to predict the future?"

"You become the observer," Jesus replied.

"Well" said Jesus, "you are not your thoughts, nor your body for that matter, but right now let's concentrate on your thoughts. You are a spark of the Divine, which is my Father/Mother/Source/Spirit. This part of you is infinite, there is no end, you will always be, and you are here on earth as a spiritual being having a human experience. Therefore, how could you possibly be your thoughts? You were in existence before you came here, from a Higher Realm and once you pass over to that Higher Realm, you will return."

I was puzzled and Jesus saw this look on my face. "So, I will always be?" I asked.

"Yes" Jesus replied. "Your true essence will always be and you may come back to earth many times to have new experiences and learn from them. It is in the learning and remembering your connection to Source that finally leads you home."

"So, how do I keep from thinking all these unhelpful thoughts then? Do I simply observe other things?"

"Yes, and observe yourself when you find yourself worrying or over-thinking. Imagine you are coming out of your body and simply be the observer of yourself. Look at yourself and be aware of what you are thinking. Then be aware of the feelings and the behaviours. Once you do this, you can choose to change these thoughts as you can clearly see you are not what you think. In changing the thought and coming back to the present moment, you can also change the feelings and behaviours as well. Happy thoughts and feelings such as gratitude will change the unhelpful thoughts too. But always remember, you, your true essence, that Divine Spark, is much more than Peter, the fisherman, son, husband, father and friend. It is your soul, you always exist and will do long after Peter's body has died and been recycled into the earth."

"I find this hard to comprehend Jesus," I replied. "So, when I was born into this body, I always was already, in a Higher Realm?"

"Yes, that's correct Peter."

"So why don't I remember, why can't I see that part of my being? Why does God have it so we forget?"

"Well, you are here to have a human experience. You are a spiritual being and to have a truly human experience you have to be able to totally embrace it and the remembering comes through silence, meditation and prayer. When you are close to God and you feel that blissful presence that is so familiar, that's when you remember that this feeling is part of you and that you are a Divine Spark - so part of God/Source/Spirit."

"But what if people don't meditate, be silent, or pray? Will they ever get that sense of remembering who they really are, that Divine Spark?" I asked.

"They may and they may not," he replied. "They may, through giving back and through kind deeds, and in moments of pure love, but most people who do these things also find time to be quiet and go within. If people choose not to go within, they go without, it's as simple as that."

"Go without what?" I asked.

"Go without connecting to their Higher Selves, the Divine Spark, the God within. Every baby is born with this. Babies have no fears, beliefs, or attitudes. They are in the present moment and pure love. They have just left the Higher Realms, so they can see and hear what the rest of you can't even connect to. Their innocence keeps them closest to God. Then life changes as they begin to walk and talk and are influenced by behaviour and the beliefs of their parents, peers and school. Children, though still very connected, lose the closeness as they grow up, unless they can be silent, appreciate nature, pray and take time to go within and spend time with their Higher Selves/God within/the Divine Spark."

"I hear you Jesus," I replied. "But it's all seems very complicated."

"I ask you now, Peter," he said, "what is complicated about spending time alone and connecting with the Source energy that created you? This Source energy - God - can guide you through this earthly lifetime, if you only listen. It's easy, it's simple, and it makes sense. If only people would listen to their souls, life would be much more pleasurable, calm and rewarding because they would be coming from Source - pure unconditional love.

Peter's Message
Time to Stop, Breathe, and Connect with Source

In this chapter Jesus is so clear about what we as humans must do, which is to always remember that we are not our thoughts. In today's world, there are so many distractions outside ourselves that take us away from going within and connecting deeply with who we truly are.

Instant gratification from social media, instant ordering and receiving and no need to wait for anything, even a TV series you like, can be viewed straight away instead of waiting the next week. This way of the world today leaves people impatient and constantly looking for the next fix, whether it be validation or in the form of material things.

It's time to stop, time to breathe, time to reconnect with Source, time to deeply go within, before it's too late.

A lifetime of searching for meaning of purpose and why you came here, what you have to give to the world, and what lessons you have to learn, are worth their weight in gold, compared to anything else you may accumulate or achieve in your lifetime.

You are not your thoughts, your body, your knowledge, status or your material possessions. You are pure unconditional love and Light. The question is, when are you going to remember this?

CHAPTER 16

Passing Over

Jesus loved to spend time with his mother, Mary. She was such a gentle woman. No wonder God had chosen her. When he was in her company, you could feel the love, admiration and deep respect that emanated from both of them and to each other.

Our children, Joshua and Maria were so in love with Jesus and Mary. They both squealed in delight when they saw them and showed such signs of affection too. One evening after supper we were all talking quietly about our day and Joshua said, "Mother Mary, what was Jesus like when he was a little boy?"

Mary smiled. "He was just like you Joshua, a delightful boy, always smiling and being very kind and helpful to others."

Joshua, delighted with the praise, added, "was he ever a bit bold, even a little tiny bit?"

Jesus was laughing now. "Well mother, was I?" he asked.

"Well there were times I did get fearful by your actions as you would just go and do your own thing, and I wouldn't know where you were or what you were doing, but it was always something where you had followed your heart and you were never in danger. As your mother though, it is a duty to look after one's children, to protect them from harm. Deep down I knew you would not come to harm but I would still worry until I found you."

"Where did Jesus go that made you worry?" Joshua asked.

"Well, we lost him in the market place once. When his father Joseph and I found him, he was chatting with the elders and he told us *'we should have known he would come to no harm.'* And when he was very small, about 6 years old, he went away for hours and we found him giving food and water to a man who was living in a hedge. Again, he told us he was doing what God wants us all to do - be kind and look after others. There were many incidents like this, but I would ask him to tell me where he was going. He would reply *'when I am called, I must follow.'* It was all very profound for such a little boy, but we understood why, this was no ordinary little boy. It was the Son of God."

"Because you are the Son of God, Jesus," Joshua asked, "did you make things happen by magic in your father's workshop?"

Jesus smiled. "No, Joshua, I didn't. My father Joseph taught me the trade of carpentry and I learnt all there is to know. I practised, made mistakes, tried again, all those things any other boy would learn. My Father in Heaven wanted me to live an earthly life and I very much respected and loved my earthly father Joseph. My mother and I miss him dearly but we do know that we will meet him again."

"How do you know?" replied Joshua, who had changed his thoughts now to the afterlife instead of magic in the world of carpentry.

"Well I just do," replied Jesus. "You come from God/Source/Spirit, you are a Divine Spark of this Higher Power/the Creator, so you will always be, even when your physical body dies. Thus, the soul part of you lives forever, so when you leave this earthly plane you will connect with the souls you spent time on earth with, especially those closest to you, the family and the people you loved."

"How do people recognise each other if their bodies aren't there?" said a puzzled Joshua.

"You connect to their energies, and you know by just being with them. You can do this here on earth when someone has passed over. You can still talk to them, feel their presence, and feel their loving energy. They will send you signs too, but you must be open to receiving them. It is so comforting to have a knowing that when a loved one has passed on, they are still with you. But again, you have to be open enough, heart and soul, to believe they are.

"Can you feel your father Joseph then? Joshua asked.

"Yes, all the time. My mother can feel him too. Can't you mother?

Mother Mary smiled. "I can sense his energy. It makes me happy to know he is still around and taking care of us. He was such a caring man, who so loved Jesus and me. He looked after us so well. When he passed over I was very sad, but I know I'll see him again in the next world."

"But, how do you feel his energy, I don't understand?" said Joshua.

"Well, it's simple really," replied Mary. "I just have a knowing when he is around. There is a certain time of the day when he'd come in from his workshop for supper. Every evening at 5pm I still feel as if he's there. I also hear him talking to me. I know it's him because it's the things he used to say and it's the way he uses his words, I don't have the same words in my mind."

"Don't you miss hugging him?" said Joshua.

"Oh, of course I do Joshua, but I have to accept that his physical presence is no longer with us, so knowing he is around is enough."

"So, does that mean you don't have to be afraid to die?" Joshua asked.

"You never have to be afraid of dying, Joshua," Jesus said. "Because you never die. You always were and always will be.

You just leave the path and continue your journey in the Light, your journey home."

Maria who had been sitting on my knee all this time and listening intensively, suddenly asked, "does going home mean there is a father and mother there to look after you and put you to bed?"

We all smiled. "Maria that is a great question!" Mary replied. "I'll let Jesus answer that one."

"All I can tell you Maria is that going home to Father/Mother of Creation is indeed a going back to where you belong and the joy of being there is like no other. You'll not need to go to bed as you'll be smiling and happy all of the time, in a blissful state that needs no earthly sleep."

"Oh, that's fine then," said Maria, "I'll like that we can play all the time Joshua, it will be lots of fun. And you can play too mother and father." Then she added, "will there be a boat for father to go fishing?"

"Your father won't need a boat for fishing in the next world as he will not need to provide for his family. Unlike earth, everything we need in the Higher Consciousness is already there. And all we need is love, that's all we ever need."

Mary smiled at her son. She was so proud of him and she beamed when he spoke. He was the same when she was in his company. The gentleness and love that was felt when they were both around was so real it could not be ignored.

Peter's Message
Death Is Not To Be Feared. We Return Home to God

Parents, their love and death, are part of life. Some parents show their love, others possess it, but do not know how to show it. Those who are incapable of unconditional love for their children are in great pain themselves and never felt that love growing up.

Jesus' love for his mother Mary and father Joseph was true and deep and unconditional. His love was the same for me and my family, and later, the Apostles, and anyone he came into contact with - always. He never judged others, he always treated everyone with such kindness and respect. He saw a Light within everyone that connected them with his Father. He saw God in all of us, because that is what we all are and within us all is that Divine Spark. We are all God. We are all connected. We are all unconditional love.

Death, too, is but a passing over. It is not to be feared. After all, you are only returning home, back to where you came from, back to that place of bliss, of knowing that only love is real and that everybody and everything in the Universe is connected.

Why humans fear death, we do not understand. Yes, it is the unknown, but there have been enough stories now of people who have had near death experiences. They always return to tell the tales of how they felt absolute peace and they felt the draw of a beautiful Light guiding them home, returning back to that place of bliss - knowing that only love is real and that everybody and everything in the Universe is connected.

In today's world there are many who are awaking to find their path in Higher Consciousness, preparing themselves and others to live on earth in a state of unconditional love. There are still many, however, who fear death, portray hate instead of love, and do not believe that God/Source/Spirit/the Universe has their back if they only surrendered to it.

You may say, "it was easy for Jesus, sure he was the Son of God. He knew God had his back, why would you forsake your own son?" Yet look at the crucifixion. Strange as that may seem, when Jesus - as a man - was at his darkest hour, his redemption arises in his resurrection, as through pure unconditional love, he forgives all sins.

Richness

Living on earth for Jesus was an honour, as he once told me. He loved the experience, and in addition to his connections with people (and especially those close to him), he enjoyed nature. He was very curious and fascinated with the land, the sea, rivers, plants, animals and birds.

One day he asked Joshua and Maria would they like to plant some vegetables and flowers and watch them grow. The children were very excited indeed. Jesus went to the market, purchased the seeds and brought them home for them, along with pots and soil.

"I've never done this before," said Joshua.

"How long will it take?" said Maria. "Can we have the vegetables for supper? Will they be ready by then?"

"No!" said Jesus laughing. "They need to grow first and that takes time. We can't force nature, everything grows in perfect time. And here we'll nurture them and give them love."

"Wonderful!" exclaimed Maria. "How will we do that?" "I'll show you," said Jesus.

So, the three of them set about their planting. Jesus showed the children how to fill the pots with soil and how to plant the seeds. They talked freely and I brought them out drinks and fresh bread during this productive lesson of sowing seeds and love.

The children loved asking Jesus questions and he loved their innocence, which he would say was so Godlike, like they were still *'home.'* Maria, in particular, was so inquisitive. Joshua, of course, would ask questions too, but he was becoming more logical about things, compared to Maria's intuitive nature.

"So, Jesus…," said Maria, "did God make these seeds?" as she popped one into the soil and then put her soil finger through her hair.

"Lovely hair, Maria," Jesus said laughing, "you'll be growing flowers in it soon with all that soil you got in there."

"Oh, that would be so beautiful," replied Maria. "Can you give me some seeds and I'll put them in now. I'd love to grow flowers in my hair."

"Don't be silly," said Joshua, "you can't really do that, can you Jesus?"

"Well no," said Jesus. "But it would be fun, wouldn't it! Maria, I tell you what we'll do. We'll plant the seeds in a pot, Maria's flowerpot. You'll take loving care of them, water, feed and nurture the seeds as they sprout and grow. Then, when they are beautiful flowers and ready to cut, you can make a flower band for your hair. How does that sound?"

"Oh, that sounds lovely," shrieked Maria. "But I may not want to cut them after all, would that not be killing them?"

"No" said Jesus, "from those flowers, others will grow, but I know what you mean. You can keep them in the pot if you want to. It will be your choice, Maria."

"What does choice mean?" asked Maria.

"Oh, I know," piped in Joshua, "it means you get to choose, to pick or decide what you want or need to do."

"Yes" said Jesus, "that's correct, Joshua. Choice is a great word and we have lots of choices in life. God my Father gave man and woman free will, and each individual has a choice every moment of every day of how to be in the world - even if they are being told what to do by someone else - they have a choice whether they have thoughts and feelings of fear, or thoughts and feelings of love."

"Oh, I choose love!" said Maria, "I love, love, love, don't you, Jesus?"

Jesus smiled, "oh, of course I do Maria, and that's what God wants for all of us, to live our lives in love, to love ourselves, to love each other, to love our land, to have gratitude for all that we have and all that we do. We are here to live with love in our hearts."

"So then, why would people live in fear?" said Joshua. "Why would they want to?"

"Well," replied Jesus, "people have fear for survival. If you were in a forest and a big scary animal was running after you, you would be scared and this fear of being killed would make you run for cover so that you could hide and be safe."

"Are you ever afraid, Jesus?" Joshua asked. "No," he replied. "Absolutely not, but that's not to say that I'll never be. I may have some fear one day, but I have a feeling it will be fleeting."

"What does fleeting mean?"

"That it won't last long," Jesus replied. "I know I am here on earth for a reason and I have to live and feel the emotions while I am here and fear is one of those emotions that all human beings have, and it intensifies as they grow. Did you know that as a baby, you were only afraid of loud noises and of falling, but even if falling, you trusted your mother and father would be there to catch you or pick you up again. And this is what grown-ups forget, they forget that God does that for them. As loving Father/Mother, he catches them, or if they have to learn a lesson from the fall, he helps pick them up and get back on their feet. Many people fail to learn from their mistakes and make the same ones many times, but that is ok too. The lesson will eventually be learned with God's help and support. In learning these lessons people can then move on to a higher level of consciousness and thus a higher vibration. Fear of falling for adults, Joshua and Maria, is a must because if you do not fall, how will you rise again?"

"So, Jesus," said Maria, "its ok to fall down. That's good, because I fall all the time and I'm so glad that God will be there to help me when I'm bigger and mother and father might not be there."

"I know," replied Maria. "I'm wiser than you think."

Jesus smiled. "I have never doubted how wise you are Maria, for a little girl you have the wisdom of an old sage."

"What about me?" said Joshua, his eyes down and with a sad face. He was afraid he was being left out.

"Oh, you are incredibly wise too, Joshua, like a wise King."

"Oh goodness," said Joshua, I am like a King, Maria, and you are like an old wrinkly woman. I am richer and more powerful."

"Let me stop you there, Joshua." said Jesus. "A king with much wealth, armies and power, is no different to the old sage who lives very simply and with very little. God makes no difference in his love. It is actually easier to be closer to God, as less is more, in God's eyes. What more do we need but to have food and shelter and love. Having many riches is not a sign of greatness. Being close to nature, being still and having a heart full of love is what is applauded in being a true human being, one who is truly close to God."

"But what if I was a king who had lots of riches, Jesus, and I was really kind and helped a lot of people in my kingdom. Is that alright then to have riches?"

Jesus smiled "Yes, of course it is Joshua, yet as the wealthy king you would always have to remember that they are not your rules to keep, they are all from God, life is from God, so all that is here on earth comes from him too."

"So, why does God make some people rich and others poor?" asked Maria.

"Well, we are all rich, Maria. Everyone who comes to earth can live a rich life, even though they may not have many riches.

These people are full of awe and wonder of the world and they appreciate the simple things in life. For those who live with much gratitude, then life is good, no matter where they are and how much they have, as long as they have food, shelter and love, they are very rich. And the love may be from others but mostly they will love themselves in honouring they are a Divine Spark of God."

"So, everyone is rich then?" added Maria.

"Yes," said Jesus smiling as he said it. "They are."

Peter's Message
The Importance of Gratitude, Joy and Unconditional Love

Jesus was always very clear in his teachings that a simple life, filled with gratitude and love, was a life fulfilling our every need. He saw no need for extravagance and unnecessary material things. Wanting more and more is only looking outside of yourself, he would say. Though he did acknowledge how abundance manifested in many forms - when those who had much love and gratitude in their hearts surrendered in trusting God's love.

I witnessed how he planted seeds when he was on his ministry. He talked to the people about the importance of gratitude, joy and love, of how love is the core of everything and once this is truly realised, all life is whole. He talked of the importance of love of self, as well as love for others, and not just friends, family and people in our community, but love for those deemed to be our enemies as well. By planting these seeds through his teachings, he, of course, led by example and there are many stories in the Bible that tell us so.

Today, however, many in the world have forgotten, and the seeds planted thousands of years ago have grown, but the weeds have also pushed through. Many religions have pushed through rules which they deem to be from God, but they are not. They are man-made and the basis of their teachings does not give fruits to gratitude, joy and unconditional love, excluding certain people from congregations and judging others' faiths. Spending on lavish things and lifestyles are not what God's love is about. Now we come with messages of simplification, acceptance, much gratitude and most importantly of all, unconditional love.

Connecting

No man is an island and Jesus' connections with everyone he met made this ever poignant. Although he taught of the importance of stillness and self-love, he also taught of how mankind had to help each other in the world, again showing that the only way is that of unconditional love.

One evening we were coming back from a fishing trip. As I said before, Jesus often came out with me as he liked both to help and be at sea. He found the water so calming and loved being in nature. This certain evening, we came across a man with a cow. The cow had stopped in the middle of the road. The man was trying to move her but the heavily pregnant cow was going nowhere. She looked like she was about to give birth. As we approached, we heard him saying, "come on now, wait until we get back to the barn, it's not long to go." But the cow was not moving.

So, we stopped with him and as we did a father and son stopped too and two women and a girl who were on their way back from the market.

"Please help me dear people," the farmer said. "This is my cow and she is in difficultly and I can't lose her or this calf. My crop failed this year and they are all I have got."

We noticed the father whisper something to his son, while the woman looked at each other with frowns. It was the little girl spoke first, "what can we do to help sir?"

He smiled "Oh thank you."

"Yes," said Jesus. "What can we do? You have Peter and I, this girl and two women, this man and his son - I'm sure with 5 adults and one teenager and a young girl that we can assist you."

It was the man who turned to Jesus and said, "I don't know if we can."

"And why not?" said Jesus, astonished.

"Well," he said in a whisper, "this man is a Pharisee - we do not mix with them. They are not our people."

The two women nodded. "Our husbands would not be pleased." One replied, "my sister and I and my daughter should be on our way."

It is not often I saw Jesus angry, but, on this occasion, his whole body language changed. This kind and gentle man, stood tall and his whole demeanour changed. "So," he said, "you would rather walk on by and this leave this man here to struggle, when you could all help in some way. You would walk away and let this cow and calf die, and this man and his family go hungry, as he has no means of supporting them!"

The man stared at Jesus, defiant in his stare. The women hung their heads. It was the little girl and then the young boy who spoke up. "I'll help if I can," she said, "I've helped my father with calving, I know what to do."

"I can help too," said the boy, "I can run fast. I could go for help." His father stared at him. "I didn't give you permission," he said. "These people do not help us, they are not one of us, why should we help him?"

Jesus then went over to the farmer and put his arm around the man. The man had tears in his eyes. "I can't afford to lose my best cow and her calf. I would help any of you if I was passing and saw you in this position."

"No man is an island," said Jesus, "we are here to help each other, and especially in times of need, and this is a time of need. Do onto others as you as you would like to be treated yourselves. I know none of you would like to be standing here today and people walk past you just because you are not 'one of theirs.' There is no such thing, because in God's eyes, we are all one." With his pure presence, the Light emanated from him and all those standing there felt calm and serene.

The two women at once hunkered down and attended to the cow. The man and his son held the cow at the head, with the boy stroking the animal and telling her she would be fine. The little girl said, "what will I do?"

"You can assist with the birth," Jesus replied, "what a wonderful task to assist with a new life coming into the world."

The farmer was overwhelmed with the help and kept saying, "thank you all so much."

"Wait until all is well," Jesus said, "which it will be." At that point he placed his hands on the cow's belly, she groaned and then was calm. Light was pouring out of Jesus' hands. Everyone was in awe.

Then the little girl cried out, "I see the calf coming!" She helped it, the farmer too. Soon after they delivered not one but two calves, much to the surprise and joy of the farmer.

"No wonder she was in difficulty," he said, "I had no idea there were two to birth. If it wasn't for you all and this Holy Man, I would not be in this position now, with a healthy cow and two healthy calves. I indeed feel very blessed." He used water from his water bottle, washed his hands, dried them on a cloth and then shook the hands of everyone. "Words cannot express my gratitude for you," he said, "especially for you two," he said, looking at the little girl and young boy.

Jesus was beaming. "How do you all feel?" he said.

"Really good," said the woman, and her sister nodded.

"I feel really happy," said the little girl, "I helped the twin calves come into the world, their mother is well and everyone is thankful. It's joyful to help others and it does not matter who they are or where they come from. It's the doing of the helping that just makes it feel wonderful."

Jesus smiled. "Yes," he replied, "the doing or the helping is what it's all about."

"I must apologise," said the man with the son. "What I said was wrong, I was judging you," he looked at the farmer. "I too am a farmer and I would not have liked to be in your position and you or anyone else pass me because we are not from the same country. Like Jesus the Holy Man said, we are all the same, it is only now I am truly seeing that. I will never again act this way to any other. From this day on, I will appreciate that we are all one."

"Apology accepted," said the farmer. "As a thank you, would you all like to come back to my house for supper?"

"Thank you," said the woman with the daughter. "But my husband is expecting us back home and my sister has to get back too. Another time."

"Oh please?" said her daughter. "Can we go soon as I want to see how the calves are doing."

The mother asked if the farmer would mind.

"Of course not!" replied the farmer. "And please bring your husband too. I want to thank him and tell him how his wife and daughter helped save my cow and calves."

Jesus and I stood back as all this talking was going on. We observed and basked in the bliss of it all. It was such a different scene from when we had arrived.

"Look at you all now," said Jesus, "you are all smiling, talking with ease and comfortable in each other's company. The energy among you all has changed, you have all raised your vibration." "You," he said looking at the little girl, "did not have to change yours as it was, and is already high, loving and trusting."

"So, let me ask you," he said, looking at the man and his son, "at what point did you decide to take a change of heart and help the farmer? What was the moment that swayed you to make another decision, so different from your original choice?"

"Well," said the man, "when you said to us *'treat others as you like to be treated yourself.'* In that instant I thought, what if it was me or my son walking with one of our cows? And it was the only one and our family depended on it. I would like it that strangers, even if they were from another community, stopped to help me or my son, I would like to be treated kindly in my time of need."

Jesus nodded and smiled. "And you?" he said to the two women, "when did you decide to not worry about what your husbands would say and make your own decision to stay and help."

"At that same moment," said the women with the daughter. "I thought if it was me here, I would expect people to stop because this is the only thing to do. It would be selfish and unkind not to, so why wouldn't I do it! it seems absurd really. Plus, why would I even consider what my husband would say? I have my own free will and I know right from wrong, and to walk on by would be wrong for everyone."

Then her sister added, "and why would we leave this poor animal in pain and distress? We not only have to treat others as we expect to be treated ourselves, but we must treat animals with respect too. To assist in the birth of her calves was a blessing.

"I am indeed humbled by all this talk," said Jesus. "However, I do hope and pray that this is not all just talk and that you will carry on these thoughts and feelings from today. It is all very well to help others, especially those we deem as different to us, or our so-called enemies, in times of crisis or great need, but this does not just need to be in these times, it must be all of the time. It is by treating others as we like to be treated ourselves, continually, no matter what - this is how we live our lives fully and in communion with God."

The little girl went over to Jesus, took his hand, looked up into his eyes and said "You are God, aren't you?"

Jesus smiled and replied, "dear one, you are very intuitive and a beautiful soul. I am God's son, here on earth, to help lead the way to the truth and Light. I will start my teaching soon, until then I ask you all to please keep this to yourselves. I will be going public soon enough and would like some more time to live quietly in the village. When I pick my Apostles, then you all can follow. Until then, live in the Light, treat everyone and every living thing with respect and most of all unconditional love."

They all departed, full of love, joy and peace, wishing each other well until they met again. As the young boy walked away he called back to Jesus, "thank you God's son, I will never forget you. I will always remember *'no man is an island.'*"

"No woman is either!" piped up the little girl, who was walking in the other direction. Jesus held out his arms and replied "Love, Love, Love!"

Peter's Message
Believing We Are Divine Sparks of God, and Being Love

Throughout his life here on earth, Jesus says no one is separate from the Divine. Everyone, he would say to me, comes from a Divine Spark from the Creator, and the Creator God cannot be explained and seen, but just is. This Higher Intelligence is part of all of us, always - always was and always will be.

"You are God, Peter." He would say.

"Me?" I'd reply, "I am not worthy."

"That's what you may think Peter. You, the villagers, the Pharisees, the Gentiles - everyone ignores their true essence which is their Light, which is God. And by doing this, they see themselves as being separate, separate from each other, and most of all, separate from God. By seeing themselves separate from each other, they then judge others, viewing them as either inferior or superior to themselves, which makes them feel above or below them. This, of course, causes rifts in communities and societies which leads to unrest, conflicts and wars."

I asked Jesus, "but how Lord, how do people break down these notions of being separate?"

"Firstly," Jesus replied "these are not notions, Peter, they are real. People truly believe they are separate from both others and God. They cannot comprehend how they could be the same or one with someone who has such opposing views to them or maybe has less money or land than they do. The very idea of this seems absurd."

"So, how Jesus, how do we break this small-minded thinking, and expand so we are in a place of acceptance and truth?"

"It is very simple, Peter," Jesus replied. "All anyone has to do is believe and love. Believe that they are Divine Sparks of God, believe it every moment of every day, and in all that they do and say. And love others because they too possess that Divine Spark that they have. It is awareness that brings this to the forefront, Peter. The world must awaken to the knowing, the knowledge, that this is the truth, the whole truth, that we are all one and only love is real. Everything else is an illusion.

In today's world there is much terror, greed, conflict, wars and tragedies which seem unexplainable. Why - many are asking - does a loving God let this all happen? Jesus talked to me of this too, of how the world in years to come would be awakening, even though simultaneously many wars and terrorists' attacks would be happening all around the world. Happening at the same time in these times of tragedy is its polar opposite - awakening more outpourings of love which shows everyone in their true colours, in their true essence, which is that of love and Light, of being truly connected to their Divine Spark, which is God.

CHAPTER 19

God Is Within

We come to the last chapter of this scribed story. This information is from me, Peter, St Peter, friend and Apostle of our Lord Jesus Christ. Many of my letters may be read and studied, along stories of me in the Bible, but until now no one has heard the real truths about how Jesus lived in his twenties, and before he started his ministry. These truths I pray will be read all over the world, so that people will know the true meaning of God's love - unconditional love - for all those who choose to believe it is so.

Those years spent as Jesus' friend were magical. Our working together to support each other's businesses, our spending time out fishing, with our loved ones, our adventures together - they all planted seeds of love and loyalty which led me to be Jesus' closest and right-hand man in relation to the Apostles, and later taking Jesus' teachings to other lands.

Our bond was so special, that when he eventually left the earth, I was in deep grief, although I felt his presence around me and knew, of course, that I would see him again.

The night before his 30th birthday, we sat outside in the moonlight, the stars were twinkling and there was such a calming presence around us. "My goodness," I said, "can you feel that, the energy surrounding us is so beautiful. I feel blissful."

"Yes" replied Jesus. "It's my Father. He has sent this loving energy to give us strength for what is to come."

"Well, as you know, we will be spreading the word, the word of God, the truth and Light. Many will welcome it, but many will not. We will be viewed by some as Holy Men. We will be viewed by others as blasphemers and fakes. Those who want to hear what we have to say will love the news and tell others who will follow. Those who fear this following will try to destroy me and our teachings."

I can remember becoming upset.

"Please do not say these things, Jesus!" I exclaimed. "This cannot be so. God would not let anything happen to you, you are his only Begotten Son." "I am, Peter" he replied, "that is why I am here, to pave the way, to remind people why they are here, to be Godlike and live life with unconditional love for themselves and others."

I had no idea then what was ahead of us. Jesus did, of course. He told me after the resurrection that he knew of every day, moment and detail because his Father/God/Source/Spirit had sent him a vision of what was to come. He had assured Jesus that this was what he had signed up to from birth, and that his coming to earth, his teachings, his actions and even in being put to death and rising again, would all bring great solace to people all over the world in the years to come.

Being naïve to all the joy Jesus' teachings would bring to many, and the hurt it would cause also to many who chose not to, or who perceived it that way, I asked Jesus "why now? Why wait until now, when you are 30 years old, to go and tell people about who you really are and why you are here? Why did you not do this 10 or 15 years ago? You were a mature boy Jesus, you could have been teaching from the age of fifteen?"

"It was not my purpose then," Jesus said. "It was my purpose to live like a boy and then a young man.

I had to live here and be here, not just be passing through and become a Holy Man with no experience of how it is to be, just to be, and do, here on earth. I have enjoyed this, Peter. I have cherished this time with my parents and so thankful for them taking such good care of me. It would not have been easy at times, especially with Herod and his men after me. I have made friends, met interesting people, connected with animals and nature, and gained valuable skills and knowledge. In fact, it has been most inspiring this journey on earth."

"Well, I hope this journey will continue for many years," I replied. Of course, unknown to me, it would only be 3 more years on earth.

"Peter, on earth, the journey will end soon enough - I know sooner than you would like, or that anyone would expect. However, after I truly leave, my story will be told and taught for thousands of years. It will be the basis for many on how to live their lives. It will be a guideline of how to live life, with the intention of living like I did, connected to God. I might add though, that these writings will be written by men, who have their own interpretations on things and some, and many, will convey stories and messages that suit their own personal moral content of how life should be lived - not the caring and unconditional love of a loving, kind, generous and forgiving God."

"But how will that happen?" I asked. "Those who know you and see you perform miracles and hear your loving teachings, how do they interpret all your work and words from God as anything but loving and forgiving?"

"Oh, those who write it all down will do so from a place of love, yet years later and through lost in translation, many of the true meanings of controversial subjects will have changed to suit those who wish to control the people. The message will be told of God who has many rules and regulations, and people will be taught to fear this God. They will be told of a burning in the flames of hell if they do not abide by them. This will keep people fearful and small and by doing so, they can be controlled. This is not as God wishes his people to love.

There will be many break-away religions along the way and many wars because of it."

"So why now teach of God's Word, the Truth and the Light, when all this will happen in the future. Is there any point?"

Jesus smiled. "Yes, Peter, there is always a point and a reason. What we will teach will be conveyed to many in later years and it will give them comfort and joy. So, the other non-truths of a fearful God, there is nothing we can do about that now. God's true presence will always be revealed to those who are willing to be open to his Divine Love and be intuitive enough to know that God is within, not a presence to be scared of.

It is when people choose to truly look within that God can fully be with them. And sometimes it is at times of darkness and challenges and/or much sadness and grief that this happens. By taking away the veil of what they were told and taught about God, they can truly explore their own thoughts and feelings, and in doing so, they find themselves. That is where they find God. And of course, that's where He/She is, or was, all along."

"So, when will we start telling people this, Jesus?" I asked.

"We have been doing it already Peter. All those people we have encountered, these past six years – the two men travelling, the young boys, the children, the women and men who did not want me to help the stranger, everyone we have met - we have impacted on their lives, and they in turn, will spread the word of a kind and loving God. The teachings we begin tomorrow, with you and the other men I have gathered to assist, will be what is recorded and used as a guide throughout the ages. Although much of this will be true recordings of what is to come, there will also be untruths that will come to cause much pain and suffering in the world. There is nothing we can do about that now Peter, we will just have to do our very best and convey the word of our loving God as we have been assigned to do."

"May I ask a question, Jesus?"

"Of course, Peter, you know you can ask me anything."

"Why, if you were so open to Sarah working in your workshop and you so value what women equally contribute to society, why is it that only men are part of our teachings team?"

"Good question, Peter." Jesus replied. "The Apostles are all men because this is acceptable in the country and culture right now, for men to travel away from their homes and families because of their work. We will be causing enough change and attention by our teachings, so to introduce women as part of the core twelve, would actually cause huge upset to many mind-sets and this would only dilute the message we are bringing to the people."

It was a bittersweet night for me, both special and sombre as I had my last night of just Jesus and myself conversing together. From then on, it was usually filled with the Apostles and disciples who, like me all those years, could not get enough of being in this energy, and hearing his words of wisdom and love.

I observed people when we travelled from town to town, as always, his pure presence simply transformed them, as if they had been hypnotised into a place of calmness and peace. They would listen to his every word, ask questions appropriately (only after he was finished speaking) and be in awe of the miracles he would perform. Many believed he was the Son of God, but those in power were threatened by his regal, yet humble presence and being, thus they would not sit back and watch this so called *'new king'* take over. Those in power knew that they could never possess what Jesus had - the attraction, the loyalty towards him from the people - which was extraordinary.

As we sat with that energy and talked about our past together, I asked questions about the future. Jesus was quick to remind me that the present moment is all that anyone ever has.

"We must teach people to appreciate this, Peter," he said. "People are so focused on past events, and either worried about or striving or looking forward to the future, that they forget to look at what they have." And even through pain and suffering, Peter, this will pass, as will joy. All these human emotions fluctuate, and being in the present gives way to acceptance for all that is."

Then we heard a noise, I looked behind me and both Joshua and Maria were standing at the door into our living quarter. "What are you two doing up?" I asked. "Were you not asleep? It's late and you have both been in bed the past three hours."

"Something's up!" Maria replied, "we can sense it." "Are you and Jesus going away?" said Joshua, with his arm around his little sister who looked as if she was about to cry.

"Come here you two," said Jesus softly. The two children walked over to Jesus and he put his arms around them both. "Listen little children," he said. "I'm not little!" said Joshua. Jesus smiled "I know Joshua, but to me, an adult, you are smaller and I mean it in a kind way. Yes, you are correct, your father and I will be going on a journey teaching about God's word, but do not fear, we will be back and forth, we are not leaving forever tomorrow morning.

"Can I come?" Joshua replied. "Me too," said Maria.

"You will both have to stay with your mother. She needs you and you need to tell the other children about Jesus and God. You will be spreading the word here among them and they will tell their parents and grandparents and other family members. You both have a very important job. God my Father says thank you."

The children were happy with Jesus' answer and they peacefully went off to bed. Sarah came in and sat with Jesus and I. The three of us sat in silence knowing big changes were ahead, and that all was well.

Peter's Message
Step Into Your Divinity and Be Unconditionally Loving

To the Scribe - It is no coincidence that this last day of scribing, for now, is on the feast day of St Peter and St Paul. I have planned for this book to be completed on this day. It is significant for all of us. It proves too that it is divinely guided. You were working to our guidelines, not your own agenda. So, on the days you did not write, or wrote very little and then beat yourself up about it, well you weren't feeling it on these days, were you? So why fight it, you were being intuitively guided by your Higher Consciousness/ Wisdom. You were being told not to. Before you came on the earth, you made a commitment to take on this honour and complete it in 4 months, finishing up on the day that is the feast day of St Peter and St Paul, so why, oh why, would it have ended any sooner?

I thank you, we thank you, for forsaking your usual busy and active business life to do this. We know it has not been easy for you as you have been conditioned to keep working and striving to build your business and watch it grow. By stopping, this goes against everything you were brought up believing to be true. You are from a strong family DNA of doers. That concept of 'just being' does not feature in your ancestral line on both sides. This is why we chose you because we knew by stopping you in your tracks - and it has been a long process - you would have to listen and you are intuitive enough to know when messages and feelings come from the High Dimensions.

Someone who may have listened too readily - say a Holy Person - may not be believed that this is true in the same way that you will be. You fit into all worlds — business, political and spiritual. Thus, people from all sectors and different interests will be willing to hear what you have to say about the experience you have had of channelling me. Many will believe it to be the truth, others will be fascinated but unsure, and as we know, many will scorn this scribing, so you have to be prepared for that.

To you, the Reader - On this day, the heavens rejoice that my true words and stories of Jesus and God's teachings are finally being told to the world. For so long I have wanted to tell these stories but the time is only right now. It is a time of great change, a time when the world may seem very grey with terrorists and tragedies, yet these events also bring such outpourings of love, sympathy, caring and kindness. A world where these individuals, communities and nations come together for the good of everyone. While hate may seem to prevail in horrendous acts, these are over-shadowed by the love and generosity shown towards those who are in grief, plus the 'hands on' financial and emotional support given by humanity. In every darkness there is Light, and Light always wins, no matter what.

When my brother Andrew and I came together with the other ten Apostles on Jesus' ministry, we were very clear about these messages of Light - God's Light, which is inside each and every one of us. We are all born with it, whether we are formally named or christened or involved in any ceremony within a religious institution or not, we ALL possess this true Light of God/Source/Spirit/the Universe as we all have a spark of the Divine - the Divine Spark is our Soul, our Higher Consciousness, our Divine Wisdom. By tapping into and truly trusting our Divine Wisdom, we then come to know our true selves, the authentic self that knows no fears, that lets go of old conditioning and limiting beliefs, and truly basks and believes in their being, their entitlement to be the I AM Presence.

2,000 years ago, we made this very clear, but through the ages, our words and teachings were changed to suit those in power, and again I state, there is no such thing as a fearful and unforgiving God. We are all God, so why would we be fearful and unforgiving towards ourselves?

In coming to an end here in these scribed words, my final message on the feast day I share with my fellow apostle and friend St Paul, is that God/Source/Spirit/the Universe is love, pure love, unconditional love. Jesus acted out what he spoke and felt, he walked the talk. Throughout the ages, in many religions, walking the talk has been sorely forgotten, thus this book will be a source of information and guide on how Jesus, God and the Higher Realms, expect you to live in peace and in harmony and unconditional love for yourself and others.

Have compassion for those who are not yet ready to live here in the Light, they will one day live a life of love.

In the meantime, be gentle with yourselves, live simply, laugh, be grateful for everything (even the hardships), be kind, spend time in nature, don't judge others or yourself, listen to your intuition, live purposefully and most of all LOVE, LOVE, LOVE.

Thank you for completing scribing, on this great day.
Now celebrate.
Love,
St Peter xo
29th June 2017

About the Author

Denise Devlin, a business women and Founder of the training and coaching company Positive Parties *'Training With A Difference'* was stopped in her *'busy'* tracks in 2016, and due to ill health, had to slow down.

It was during this time of being still, one day at the end of February 2017, when she was journaling, she asked the questions: "What wisdom do you have that can help me right now? What part longs to step forward right now? What part of me is ready to emerge?" Immediately her right arm started moving uncontrollably and the pen scribbled all over the page.

This was the beginning of the channelling from St Peter. There were many signs of reassurance, relating to the date the 18th November that led Denise on this journey of scribing for St Peter, but that is another story.

Although torn between the business and corporate worlds and her spiritual path of channelling this book, Denise was tested to the point that nothing would flow until this book was published. Having hope, trust and faith, Denise continues to plant the seeds of spiritual awareness and unconditional love both in the business world, public sector, education sector and communities and in the books she scribes. This is her first channelled book, another one is in progress.

Denise lives in the hills above Strabane, Northern Ireland with her husband Neil, 2 daughters, Emer & Orla, Chico the border collie, Marmalade the cat, Christophe the rooster and the 4 hens – Henny Penny, Chicken Licken, Cynthia and Fluffy Pants. ☺

For further information about Denise Devlin and the story behind channelling this book, go to www.thegapyears.com

04160766-00955638

Printed in the United States
By Bookmasters